Preces Ecclesiasticae

PRECES ECCLESIASTICÆ.

The Forms of Public Devotion,

INSTITUTED BY

CALVIN, JOHN KNOX, MARTIN BUCER, MICRONIUS,

AND OTHER PRESBYTERIAN DIVINES;

ADOPTED AND USED IN

Various Branches of the Presbyterian Church.

NEWLY COLLECTED AND COLLATED.

NEW YORK:

CHARLES SCRIBNER, 145 NASSAU STREET.

1856.

In adducing these Forms of Worship, set forth by the Reformers at an early period in the history of the Presbyterian Church, it is designed to solicit a critical examination of them on the part of individuals to whose notice this Collection may come. The want of a Formulary of Public Services, for the optional use and study of the Clergy, as well as for the assistance of Congregations in localities where the stated Ministry of the Gospel is not enjoyed, has been both felt and expressed; and the present Compilation has no other purpose than to promote and facilitate the preparation of such a work, based as it must be upon the old materials, with additions and modifications to be suggested by brethren of experience. Accordingly, this Compilation is sent forth for gratuitous circulation, among a limited number of those who are supposed to feel interest in the object; whilst it is withheld from general publicity, in order that such emendations as shall appear demanded, may be privately obtained. The free communication of any suggestions of this nature, is respectfully and earnestly requested, from each of those who shall receive this pamphlet.

In the preparation of this work, the entire literature of the subject has been studied, beginning with Calvin's "PRECES ECCLESIASTICÆ," the title of which has been adopted, and proceeding through the several formularies founded upon that admirable basis: those, namely, of the Churches of Geneva, France, Scotland, Holland, the Palatinate, Germany, Hungary, French Switzerland, and the Valleys of Piedmont. Many of the Forms here given are common to all of these rituals, whose affinity of course is strongly marked. Reference to the authorship of each will be found in the text or in the notes appended.

Large use has been made of Richard Baxter's "Reformed Liturgy"— a work which has never been sanctioned by ecclesiastical adoption, yet well deserves the careful study of every minister. The remarkable volume issued in the year 1545, under the direction of Archbishop Herman of Cologne, has also been consulted—a production of which Martin Bucer, the learned disciple of Calvin, was the principal author. Both of these liturgical performances may be justly viewed as Presbyterian by their origin.

The plan of the present work embraces, in addition to these General Forms of celebrating the Public Ordinances of Religion, a collection of Occasional and Special Prayers, derived from the same sources. To avoid an extension that would render the expense of printing too great, this part has been withheld for the time being.

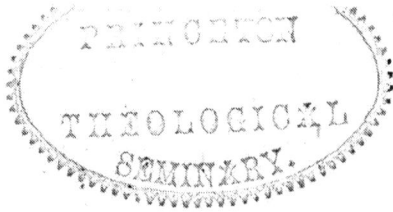

THE

ORDER OF DIVINE SERVICE

ON THE

Morning of the Lord's Day.

Preface.

Thus saith the Lord, The heaven is my throne, and the earth. is my footstool: where is the house that ye build unto me? and where is the place of my rest? For all those things hath mine hand made, and all those things have been, saith the Lord: but to this man will I look, even to him that is poor and of a contrite spirit, and trembleth at my word.

Or one of the following sentences:

Thus saith the High and Lofty One that inhabiteth eternity, whose name is Holy: I dwell in the high and holy place, with him also that is of a contrite and humble spirit, to revive the spirit of the humble, and the heart of the contrite ones.

Thus saith the Lord, The sons of the stranger, that join themselves to the Lord, even them will I bring to my holy mountain, and make them joyful in my house of prayer: their burnt-offerings and their sacrifices shall be accepted upon mine altar; for mine house shall be called an house of prayer for all people.

Thus saith the Lord, In all places where I record my name I will come unto thee, and I will bless thee.

Our Lord Jesus Christ hath said, Where two or three are gathered together in my name, there am I in the midst of them: and whatsoever ye shall ask in my name, that will I do.

Christ is not entered into the holy places made with hands, which are the figures of the true; but into heaven itself, now to appear in the presence of God for us.

Invitation.

Having therefore this promise, dearly beloved, let us draw near with a true heart, in full assurance of faith, and make known our requests unto God.

Or:

Let us, therefore, come boldly unto the throne of grace, that we may obtain mercy, and find grace to help in time of need.

THE OPENING PRAYER.

Invocation and Confession of Sins.

I.

Almighty God! who hast promised to be present with Thy people, and to grant their requests in the name of Thy well-beloved Son: look down, we beseech Thee, upon us, and for the sake of Him who is our only Saviour and Mediator with Thee, fulfil Thy promise in our behalf: that our thoughts being lifted up, and our desires drawn forth unto Thee, we may seek Thee acceptably this day: Through Jesus Christ our Redeemer.

Eternal God! we acknowledge and confess before Thy sovereign Majesty that we are miserable sinners, conceived and born in guilt, prone to evil, unable of ourselves to do any good. We have broken Thy laws in thought, word, and deed, deserving most justly Thy wrath and condemnation. But we repent and are sorry for our offences; we humble ourselves at Thy throne, and beseech Thee to regard us in Thy great compassion. Have mercy upon us, O God! Father of Mercies, for the sake of the holy life and sufferings of Thy dear Son our Saviour, Jesus Christ. Pardon all our sins, blot out our transgressions, renew us wholly, and grant us the continual help of Thy Holy Spirit. May He deliver us more and more from the power of sin, that we may present ourselves living sacrifices unto Thee, and serve Thee without fear all our days, to the honour of Thy Name and our salvation: Through Jesus Christ our Lord and Saviour. Amen.   CALVIN.

II.

O Eternal, Almighty, and Most Gracious God! Heaven is Thy throne and earth is Thy footstool: holy and reverend is Thy Name. We sinners are bold, through our blessed Mediator, to present ourselves and our supplications before Thee. Receive us graciously, help us by Thy Spirit, let Thy fear be upon us, let Thy word come unto us in power and be received in love; cause us to be fervent in prayer, and joyful in thy praises, and to serve Thee this day without distraction, that we may find it good for us to draw near unto Thee. BAXTER.

Most Holy God! who art of purer eyes than to behold iniquity, who condemnest the ungodly, impenitent, and unbelieving, but hast promised mercy through Jesus Christ unto all that repent and believe in Him: We confess that we were conceived in sin, and are by nature children of wrath, and have all sinned and come short of the glory of God. Thou hast revealed unto us Thy wonderful love in Christ, and offered us pardon and salvation in Him: but we have resisted Thy Spirit, and neglected so great salvation; we have run into temptations; and the sin we should have hated we have committed in Thy sight, both secretly and openly, ignorantly and carelessly, rashly and presumptuously, against Thy promises, Thy mercies, and Thy judgments. Our transgressions are multiplied before Thee, and our sins testify against us; if Thou deal with us as we deserve, Thou wilt cast us away from Thy sight. Have mercy upon us, O God! be reconciled unto us, and let the blood of Jesus Christ cleanse us from all our sins. Take us for Thy children, and give us the Spirit of Thy Son. Oh! make Thy face to shine upon Thy servants; save us from our sins, and from the wrath to come; make us a peculiar people to Thee, zealous of Thy praise. We ask it in the name of our blessed and only Redeemer. Amen. BAXTER.

III.

Most Gracious God, our Heavenly Father! in whom dwelleth all fulness of light and wisdom: Illuminate our minds by Thy Spirit, in the true understanding of Thy Word, and the right worship of Thy name; dispel the darkness of our corrupt nature, and dispose us to commune with Thee through the Spirit of grace and supplication. Help us to put our whole trust in Him alone by whose merits we approach Thee; and since Thou art pleased for His sake to number us among Thy people, make us able and willing to pay Thee acceptable worship, as children to our Father, and obedient servants to our King. CALVIN.

We are not worthy, O Lord! to come into Thy presence, by reason of our manifold offences. For we were conceived in sin, and in iniquity was every one of us born. All the days of our life we have continued to follow the corruption of our fleshly nature. If Thou, Lord, shouldst enter into judgment with Thy servants, just occasion hast Thou to punish not only this our mortal flesh, but our bodies and souls for ever. But Thou, O Lord! art a merciful God, a loving and favourable Father, to all that unfeignedly turn unto Thee from their sins. Wherefore we most humbly beseech Thee, for the sake of Christ, Thy Son, shew Thy mercy upon us. Forgive us all our offences. Endue us with Thine Holy Spirit. Sanctify us wholly; and grant us grace, that in all the days of our lives hereafter, we may study to serve and please Thee, in word and in deed, through our only Lord and Master, Jesus Christ. Amen. KNOX.

IV.

Eternal and Invisible God! Infinite in power, wisdom, and goodness, dwelling in the light which no man can approach, yet dwelling also with the humble and contrite, and taking pleasure in Thy people : Thou hast consecrated for us a new and living way, that with boldness we may enter into the holiest by the blood of Jesus. Behold us at Thy footstool. Despise us not, though unworthy; put Thy fear into our hearts, that with reverence we may serve Thee; write Thy laws in our minds, and let us all be taught of Thee. So may the words of our mouths and the meditations of our hearts be acceptable in Thy sight, through Jesus Christ our Redeemer. BAXTER.

Almighty, Everlasting God! Father of our Lord Jesus Christ! Creator of all things, Judge of all men! We acknowledge and lament in Thy sight, that we were conceived and born in sin, prone to evil, and unfit for any good. We have broken Thy holy laws, times and ways without number, by contempt of Thee and Thy Word, by distrust of Thy grace, and vain confidence in ourselves and the world, by thoughts and works grievously offending Thy holy Majesty, and sinning against our neighbour. Thus have we buried ourselves more and more deeply in spiritual death. But we do earnestly repent, and are sorry for these our misdoings. Have mercy upon us, most Gracious and Merciful Father, for the sake of Thy Son, Jesus Christ our Lord. Forgive us all that is past. Grant us and increase within us Thine Holy Spirit; who shall teach us penitently to acknowledge our sins, and being touched with lively sorrow, by true faith to obtain remission of them in Christ. So that daily dying unto sin, in newness of life we may serve and please Thee, to the glory of Thy name and the edification of Thy Church: Through Jesus Christ our Lord. Amen. BUCER.

Then may be read THE COMMANDMENTS, *recorded in Exodus, chapter XX., verse 1 to 17: Instead of which sometimes* THE BEATITUDES, *from the Gospel of St. Matthew, chapter V., verse 1 to 10.*

Then follows the singing of a PSALM *or* HYMN *of Praise and Thanksgiving.*

Next the READING OF SCRIPTURE, *out of the Old and New Testaments.*

Then let the minister say:

Let us pray.

THE GENERAL PRAYER.

Beginning with the prayer of Our Lord.

Our Father which art in heaven, Hallowed be Thy name. Thy kingdom come. Thy will be done in earth, as it is in heaven. Give us this day our daily bread. And forgive us our debts, as we forgive our debtors. And lead us not into temptation, but deliver us from evil: For Thine is the kingdom, and the power, and the glory, for ever. Amen.

Here may be introduced whatever special matter of prayer shall be thought appropriate, suited to the theme of discourse or the occasion; concluding with one of these following forms of

Supplication and Intercession.

I.

Heavenly Father, who hast bidden us pray for all in authority among men: Bless, we intreat Thee, all rulers and magistrates to whom Thou hast committed power; and especially Thy servant, the President of the United States, our governors, legislators, and judges. May it please Thee to grant them the daily increase of Thy good Spirit, that with true faith acknowledging Christ Thy Son to be King of kings and Lord of lords, they may seek to honour Thee and exalt Thy rule. May they wisely govern those who are the sheep of Thy pasture and the creatures of Thy hand; so that as well here as throughout all the world, Thy people being kept in peace and quiet may serve Thee without fear. Be pleased, O Merciful God! to look favourably upon our country. Grant unto her prosperity and peace; the permanence of her free institutions; the stability of her union; the successful growth of her agriculture, commerce, and manufactures. Let the sanctifying leaven of Thy Gospel pervade all our people: for we have no King but Thee, O God! and righteousness alone exalteth a nation.

Almighty Saviour! We pray for all Pastors and Ministers of thy Church, intrusted by Thee with the care of souls and the preaching of Thy Word. Guide them ever by Thy Spirit, and keep them faithful in their sacred charge. Give grace to all Missionaries of the Cross, that by their means Thy wandering sheep may be gathered in and made subject to the Shepherd and Bishop of their souls. Deliver Thy Church from heresy and false doctrine: and unite Thy people with one accord in the faith and practice of the Gospel.

Father of Mercies! We pray for every class and condition of our fellow-men. Thou that wouldst be acknowledged as the Saviour of all mankind, in the redemption wrought by Thy Son, Jesus Christ: grant that such as are yet strangers to Thee, and captives to ignorance and error, may be led by the enlightening of Thy Spirit and Thy Word, into the right way of salvation. Strengthen those already visited with Thy grace, that they may daily grow in godliness, being enriched with every spiritual gift. So hasten the time when all Thy creatures upon the earth, with one heart and one voice, shall fear and praise Thee, giving honour and worship to Thy Christ, our Lord, Lawgiver, and King.

God of all Comfort! We commend to Thee those whom Thou art pleased to chasten with any cross or tribulation; all people afflicted with pestilence, war, or famine; all persons oppressed with poverty, sickness, distress of body or grief of mind. May it please Thee to manifest unto them Thy fatherly kindness in all their afflictions, to the end that in their hearts they may turn unto Thee, and being converted, receive perfect consolation, and deliverance from all their woes.

Finally, O God our Father! Grant also unto us here gathered in the name of Thy Holy Child Jesus, to hear His Word, [and to celebrate His Supper,] that we may rightly perceive our lost estate by nature, and the condemnation we have deserved by disobedient lives. And conscious that in ourselves there dwelleth no good thing, and that flesh and blood can not inherit Thy kingdom, may we with our whole affections give ourselves up in firm trust to Thy beloved Son Jesus Christ, our only Saviour and Redeemer: that He, dwelling in us, may mortify all remaining sin, renewing us for that better life where we shall magnify Thy blessed Name ever, world without end.

CALVIN.

The Creed.

Lord, increase our faith.

I believe in God the Father Almighty, Maker of heaven and earth; and in Jesus Christ His only Son, our Lord; who was conceived by the Holy Ghost, born of the Virgin Mary, suffered under Pontius Pilate, was crucified, dead, and buried; He descended into hell;* the third day He rose again from the dead; He ascended into heaven, and sitteth on the right hand of God the Father Almighty; from thence He shall come to judge the quick and the dead. I believe in the Holy Ghost; the Holy Catholic Church, the communion of saints; the forgiveness of sins; the resurrection of the body; and the life everlasting. Amen.

II.

Almighty God! who by Thine holy Apostle hast taught us to make our prayers and supplications for all men: We beseech Thee to lead such as are yet in the captivity of ignorance and error, to the pure understanding of Thine heavenly truth; so that all mankind, with one consent, may learn to worship Thee their only God and Saviour. Give grace to all pastors and ministers of Thy holy Word, to whom Thou hast committed the charge of Thy chosen people, that in life and doctrine they may be found faithful, setting only before them Thy glory; and may all poor sheep that wander and go astray, by them be gathered and brought home to Thy fold.

Be pleased graciously to preserve and govern all Christian Churches throughout the earth, in unity of [true] faith, and in godliness of life. Let Thy kingdom daily increase, and that of Satan be destroyed; till Thy kingdom be perfected, when Thou shalt be all in all.

We pray for these United States; God bless our people; keep them under Thy holy protection; prosper them in their agriculture, manufactures, commerce, and literature; and let their civil and religious rights be preserved inviolate to the latest posterity.

And because the hearts of rulers are in Thine hand, we beseech Thee to guide and govern all those to whom Thou hast committed the sword. Especially, O Lord! according to our bounden duty, we intreat Thee to bless the President, his councillors, and all others in authority in this land. Let Thy fatherly favour so preserve them, let Thine Holy Spirit so direct

* *i. e.*, Continued in the state of the dead, and under the power of death, until the third day.

their minds, that they may execute their office to the maintenance of pure religion, and the punishment of evil-doers,
according to the precise rule of Thine holy Word.

And for that we be all members of the mystical body of
Christ Jesus, we make our requests unto Thee, O heavenly
Father! for such as are afflicted with any kind of cross or
tribulation, as war, plague, famine, poverty, sickness, or any
other kind of Thy chastisements, whether it be grief of body
or unquietness of mind: That it would please Thee to give
them patience and constancy, till Thou send them full deliverance out of all their woes.

And finally, O Lord God, Most Merciful Father! We beseech Thee to shew Thy great mercies upon those our brethren
who may be persecuted, cast into prison, and condemned to
death, for the testimony of Thy Truth: and though they be
utterly destitute of all man's aid, yet let Thy sweet comfort
never depart; but so inflame their hearts with Thine Holy
Spirit, that they may boldly and cheerfully abide such trial as
Thy godly wisdom shall appoint. And may all Thy afflicted
people so serve and follow Thee, that at length, as well by
their death as by their life, the kingdom of Thy Son Jesus
Christ may increase and shine throughout the world.

These graces, O Heavenly Father! and all others that Thou
knowest to be expedient for us, and for all mankind, we ask
in the name of our Sovereign Master, Christ Jesus, Thy well-
beloved Son; and for His sake also, we beseech Thee to grant
us perfect continuance in the lively faith of Thy Universal
Church, whereof we make our confession, saying:

I believe in God, etc.   KNOX.

III.

O Most Holy, Blessed, and Glorious Trinity! Father, Son,
and Holy Ghost! Three Persons and one God; our Creator,
Redeemer, and Sanctifier; our Lord, our Governor, and Father! Hear us, and have mercy upon us!

O Lord our Saviour! God and man; Who, having assumed
our nature, by Thy sufferings, death, and burial, wast made a
ransom to take away the sins of the world; who, being raised
from the dead, ascended and glorified, art made Head over
all things to the Church: We beseech Thee to hear us, and
have mercy upon us. Make sure to us our calling and election,
our unfeigned faith and repentance; that being justified and
made the sons of God, we may have peace with Him as our
reconciled God and Father.

Let Thy Holy Spirit sanctify us, and dwell in our hearts,

and cause us to deny ourselves, and to give ourselves entirely to Thee.

As the world was created for Thy glory, let Thy name be glorified throughout the world. Let self-love, and pride, and vain-glory be destroyed. Make us to love Thee, fear Thee, and trust in Thee with all our hearts, and to live to Thee.

Let all mankind subject themselves to Thee, their King. Let the kingdoms of the world become the kingdoms of the Lord, and of His Christ. Let atheists, idolators, Mohammedans, Jews, and all ungodly people be converted. Send forth meet laborers into the harvest, preserve and bless them in their work, and let the Gospel be preached throughout all the world.

Unite all Christians in Jesus Christ, the true and only universal Head, in the true Christian and Catholic faith and love. Cast out heresies and corruptions, heal divisions, let the strong receive the weak, and bear their infirmities.

Have mercy upon our rulers; let them fear Thee, and be ensamples of piety and temperance, haters of injustice, covetousness and pride, and defenders of the innocent. Let every soul be subject to the higher powers, and not resist; let them obey all in authority, not only for wrath, but for conscience' sake.

Give all Thy Churches able, holy, faithful pastors, that may soundly and diligently preach Thy Word, and guide Thy flock in ways of righteousness and peace.

Keep us from atheism, idolatry, and rebellion against Thee; from infidelity, ungodliness, and sensuality; from security, presumption, and despair.

Keep us from murder and violence, and hurtful, passionate words and actions. Keep us from fornication and all uncleanness; from stealing; from perverting justice; from false witness and deceit; from slander or uncharitable censure. Keep us from coveting any thing that is our neighbours'. Cause us to love Christ in His members with a pure and fervent love; to love our enemies, and to do good to all.

Give us needful sustenance, and contentment therewith. Bless our labours, and the fruits of the earth in their season; and give us such temperate weather as may tend thereunto. Deliver us and all Thy servants from sickness, want, or other distresses, that would hinder us from Thy service. When we sin, restore us by true repentance and faith in Christ. May we loathe ourselves for our transgressions; forgive them all, and accept us in Thy well-beloved Son. Save us from the punishment that our sins deserve, and teach us heartily to forgive others. Convert our enemies, persecutors, and slanderers, and forgive them. Cause us to watch against temptation, to resist and overcome the world, the flesh, and the devil. Deliver us and all Thy people from the enmity and rage of Satan; and preserve us to Thy heavenly Kingdom.

For Thou only art the Universal King; all power is Thine in heaven and earth; of Thee, and through Thee, and to Thee, are all things; and the glory shall be Thine for ever. Amen.

BAXTER.

I believe in God, etc.

IV.

O Lord our God, who hast commanded us to make prayers and supplications for all men, we present ourselves before Thy throne to offer up our requests in behalf of all classes and conditions of our race. Thou, Lord, who art the Maker and Father of mankind, we beseech Thee for the peace of the whole world, and the salvation of all people. Deliver from their blindness the heathen, Mohammedans, and all unbelievers; and vouchsafe according to Thy promises to procure the conversion of Thine ancient people the Jews: that all nations may know and worship Thee, and Jesus Christ whom Thou hast sent. King of kings, Lord of lords, we pray to Thee for all rulers and other persons in offices of dignity and trust. Give the knowledge of Thyself to such as have it not: and impart Thy grace to them that know Thee, that they may use their authority to the furtherance of Thy glory. Especially we pray for the President of the United States, for our governors, and for all our magistrates. Grant unto them long life and prosperity, good counsel and success. Bless the people of this commonwealth in all their interests, civil and religious. Diffuse among them the spirit of wisdom and understanding, the spirit of knowledge and the fear of Thy Name: that order and harmony may prevail, and that we may lead a quiet and peaceable life in all godliness and honesty.

We present to Thee, O Lord, our prayers for the necessities of Thy holy Church, spread abroad throughout the earth. Be pleased to protect, increase, and sanctify it more and more. Deliver the churches that are persecuted. Remove the errors, scandals, and divisions that distract Christendom, and unite all Christians by the bonds of truth, piety, and peace. Grant especially Thy blessings upon the churches of this land, and the churches in this place: bless the families composing them: cause righteousness, and all holy virtues, to flourish in our midst.

We pray Thee, O God, for all the pastors of Thy Church; sanctify them, illuminate them, and augment in them the gifts needful for the promotion of Thy kingdom, and the salvation of souls intrusted to their care. Raise up everywhere, and especially among ourselves, faithful, zealous, humble ministers, lovers of truth and of peace. And to this end impart Thy grace and Thy fear unto all that are preparing to serve Thee in the ministry of Thy Word.

O God of Mercy, have pity upon the nations that are afflicted by war, or any other scourge; and upon all persons who are in any kind of suffering. We commend to Thee the widows, the orphans, the poor, the strangers, the friendless; those that are journeying; those that endure persecution for Thy Gospel; all persons distressed or diseased in mind; the infirm, the sick, the dying; and especially our brethren who are members of this church [and who desire our prayers]. Assist them all in their several necessities, whether of body or of soul; and give them a happy issue out of all their troubles.

Lord, we beseech Thee for all Thy children: for all that seek Thee in sincerity of heart, and labour to promote their own salvation and that of their fellow-men; for all that are engaged in works of piety, and enterprises for the extension of Thy Kingdom. Confirm those that are weak in the Faith; and to all that are yet in their sins, under condemnation of Thy law, give true repentance and conversion unto Thee.

Look favourably upon this community. Grant us always that which may be needful for our sustenance; and enable us to serve Thee with sobriety, thankfulness, and love. Deliver us from our sins; preserve us from wicked thoughts, from unbelief, hypocrisy, and whatever is opposed to Thy holy will. O Merciful God, prevent us ever by Thy grace, and guide us continually by Thy Spirit; put in our minds right purposes and pure desires, perfect submission to Thy providence, fervent love to Thee, and charity that shall incline us to love and edify one another. Detach our hearts from this world of vanity, and help us to raise them to heaven, where our treasure is. So that living in watchfulness and prayer, in temperance and holiness, we may pass our days in Thy peace, waiting for the glorious appearing of our Lord: that when He shall come to judge the world, we may stand in Thy presence without shame.

Give ear, O Lord, unto the voice of those who have now offered their prayers unto Thee: reject not the unworthy supplications of Thy servants; but grant us the blessings we have asked, and all other things that are necessary for us, in the name of Jesus Christ our Lord: unto whom, with the Father, and the Holy Ghost, be honour and praise for ever. Amen.

NEUCHATEL LITURGY.

Lord! increase our faith.

I believe in God, etc.

After this prayer, let a hymn be sung before the

SERMON.

At the conclusion of which another hymn, and then one of the following prayers, or to the like effect.

THE CLOSING PRAYER.

Thanksgiving.

I.

Honour and praise be given to Thee, O Lord God Almighty, our Father, Saviour, and Sanctifier! for all Thy mercies and loving-kindnesses shewed unto us Thy people. We praise Thee for the goodness that freely chose us to salvation before the world began. We thank Thee for creating us after Thine own image; for redeeming us when we were lost, with the precious blood of Christ; for sanctifying us with Thy Spirit in the revelation and knowledge of Thy Word; for Thy help and succour in our necessities, Thy fatherly comfort in our tribulations; for saving us in dangers of body and soul, and giving us so large a time of repentance. These benefits, O most Merciful Father! we acknowledge to have received of Thine only goodness; and so do we implore Thy grace continually to augment our thankfulness toward Thee, kindling our hearts with pure and fervent love. Suffer us not in vain to receive Thy Word; but graciously assist us always, in heart, word, and deed, to sanctify and worship Thy holy Name.

And now unto the Father, unto the Son, and unto the Holy Ghost, one God, be ascribed in the Church all honour and glory, might, majesty, and dominion, henceforth and for ever. Amen.

KNOX.

II.

Most Glorious God! Accept, through Thy beloved Son, our thanksgivings for Thy unspeakable love and goodness. Thou art the Father of Mercies and the God of all Consolation, full of compassion, forgiving iniquity, transgression, and sin. For Thy glory Thou didst create us after Thine image; and when we forsook Thee, Thou didst not leave us in the hands of death, but didst so love the world as to give Thy Son to be our Saviour. We thank Thee for His death, that saveth us from death, and for His life, that opened us the way to life. We thank Thee for the new and better Covenant; for Thy great and precious promises; that Thou hast given us eternal life in Christ; that we have the clear and sure revelation of Thy will in the holy Scriptures; that Thou hast founded Thy Church upon Apostles and Prophets, Jesus Christ himself being the

head corner-stone. We thank Thee that Thou hast commu-
nicated to Thy ministers the Word of reconciliation; that by
them Thou hast opened our eyes, and turned us from darkness
unto light; that Thou hast adopted us to be Thy sons, and
joint-heirs with Christ, and made us His members, and given
us His Spirit. All Thy paths, O Lord! are mercy and truth
to such as keep Thy covenant. Oh! continue Thy loving-
kindness unto us, that we may rejoice and be glad in Thee all
our days. Guide us by Thy counsel, and afterward receive us
to Thy glory; where, with all the blessed host of heaven, we
may behold, admire, and perfectly and joyfully praise Thee,
our most glorious Creator, Redeemer, and Sanctifier, for ever
and ever. Amen. BAXTER.

III.

O Lord our God, we lift up our hearts unto Thee, in grateful acknowledgment of all Thy mercies and benefits to us.
We praise Thee as the source of all blessings, full of compassion and goodness unto the children of men. We thank Thee
that Thou hast formed us reasonable creatures, capable of
knowing and serving Thee. We bless Thee for Thy preserv-
ing care over us, and for all our temporal enjoyments. Above
all we praise Thee, O most Merciful Father, for Thy spiritual
blessings in Christ Jesus; for the Holy Spirit, and His influ-
ences; for the Covenant of Grace, and all the precious promises thereof; for Thy Word, for the Gospel ministry, and all
Thine ordinances. For these benefits we bless Thee, O God,
the Father, the Son, and the Holy Ghost; our Creator, Redeemer, and Sanctifier. And now, Lord, we commit ourselves
to Thee, we hope in Thy mercies, and we wait for Thy salvation. Accept our worship, and forgive our sins, in the name
of our crucified and exalted Redeemer, Jesus Christ: unto
whom, with the Father, and the Spirit of all Grace, be ascribed
glory, honour, dominion, and praise, for ever and ever. Amen.
DIRECTORY REVISED, 1787.

IV.

O God! Thy glory is great in all Thy Churches, and the
praises of Thy Name resound among the assemblies of Thy
saints. We thy servants would humble ourselves before Thee,
and worship Thine infinite Majesty. We celebrate Thy wisdom, power, and goodness, that shine forth in the works of
creation and redemption through Jesus Christ our Lord. We
bless Thee for all temporal and spiritual good that we continually receive at Thy bountiful hands. But more especially
with all Thy people assembled this day, we praise Thee that

Thou didst send into the world Thy Son to save us; and having delivered Him up for our offences, didst raise him again for our justification; and through His glorious resurrection hast given us the blessed hope of everlasting life. O Lord! may these our thanksgivings come up with acceptance before Thy throne. Make us worthy at the last day to have part in the resurrection of the just, and the glory of the kingdom of heaven: whither Jesus the Forerunner hath for us entered; where now He lives and reigns, and is worshipped and glorified, with Thee and the Holy Ghost, God blessed for ever. Amen.

FRENCH & WALDENSIAN LITURGIES.

Benediction.

The Lord bless thee, and keep thee:

The Lord make His face shine upon thee, and be gracious unto thee:

The Lord lift up His countenance upon thee, and give thee peace. Amen.

Or:

The grace of the Lord Jesus Christ, and the love of God, and the communion of the Holy Ghost, be with you all. Amen.

THE COMMANDMENTS,

To be read after the Opening Prayer in the Morning Service.

N. B.—That the Law of God may be heard by the people with profit, the minister should always read it in a spirit of reverence and devotion ; and it may be proper to pause after each precept, to allow the offering up of a silent petition for grace and forgiveness, which the people should be recommended to do.

I.

And God spake all these words, saying, I am the Lord thy God, which have brought thee out of the land of Egypt, out of the house of bondage. Thou shalt have no other gods before me.

II.

Thou shalt not make unto thee any graven image, or any likeness of any thing that is in heaven above, or that is in the earth beneath, or that is in the water under the earth : thou shalt not bow down thyself to them, nor serve them : for I the Lord thy God am a jealous God, visiting the iniquity of the fathers upon the children unto the third and fourth generation of them that hate me ; and shewing mercy unto thousands of them that love me, and keep my commandments.

III.

Thou shalt not take the name of the Lord thy God in vain, for the Lord will not hold him guiltless that taketh His name in vain.

IV.

Remember the Sabbath-day, to keep it holy. Six days shalt thou labour, and do all thy work : but the seventh day is the Sabbath of the Lord thy God : in it thou shalt not do any work, thou, nor thy son, nor thy daughter, thy man-servant, nor thy maid-servant, nor thy cattle, nor thy stranger that is within thy gates : for in six days the Lord made heaven and earth, the sea, and all that in them is, and rested the seventh day : wherefore the Lord blessed the Sabbath-day, and hallowed it.

V.

Honour thy father and thy mother : that thy days may be long upon the land which the Lord thy God giveth thee.

VI.

Thou shalt not kill.

VII.

Thou shalt not commit adultery.

VIII.

Thou shalt not steal.

IX.

Thou shalt not bear false witness against thy neighbour.

X.

Thou shalt not covet thy neighbour's house, thou shalt not covet thy neighbour's wife, nor his man-servant, nor his maid-servant, nor his ox, nor his ass, nor any thing that is thy neighbour's.

Response.

Which may be sung by the choir and congregation.

1 KINGS VIII., 57, 58

The Lord our God be with us: let Him not leave us nor forsake us: that He may incline our hearts unto Him, to walk in all His ways, and to keep His commandments.

Or, HEBREWS VIII., 10, 12.

Lord, put Thy laws into our mind, and write them in our hearts: be merciful to our unrighteousness, and our iniquities remember no more.

THE BEATITUDES,

To be sometimes read in place of the Commandments.

N. B.—It is proper that each of these Beatitudes be followed by the congregation with a silent petition for grace to inherit the blessing.

I.

Our Lord Jesus Christ hath said, Blessed are the poor in spirit: for theirs is the kingdom of heaven.

II.

Blessed are they that mourn: for they shall be comforted.

III.

Blessed are the meek: for they shall inherit the earth.

IV.

Blessed are they which do hunger and thirst after righteousness: for they shall be filled.

V.

Blessed are the merciful: for they shall obtain mercy.

VI.

Blessed are the pure in heart: for they shall see God.

VII.

Blessed are the peace-makers: for they shall be called the children of God.

VIII.

Blessed are they which are persecuted for righteousness' sake: for theirs is the kingdom of heaven.

Response,

Which may be sung by the choir and congregation.

PSALM LXVII., 1.

God be merciful unto us, and bless us; and cause His face to shine upon us.

THE

ORDER OF DIVINE SERVICE

ON THE

Evening of the Lord's Day.

Or, on an Evening in the Week.

[*The Presbyterian Formularies of Worship impose no special order for the second service on the Lord's Day   The original practice of those Divines who framed them was to devote that service to the catechetical instruction of the young · a practice entirely consonant with the importance always attached by the Church to that duty. Hence the Minister was left to entire freedom of selection or composition for the afternoon service of the Lord's Day. as well as for whatever occasional services might be celebrated upon week-days.   The following forms were given for voluntary use.*]

OUR help is in the Name of the Lord, who made heaven and earth.   Amen.

To this may be added one of these sentences :

Let the words of my mouth, and the meditation of my heart, be acceptable in Thy sight, O Lord, my Strength and my Redeemer.

O send out Thy light and Thy truth: let them lead me; let them bring me unto Thy holy hill, and to Thy tabernacles: Then will I go unto the altar of God, unto God my exceeding joy.

I will lift up mine eyes unto the hills, from whence cometh my help : my help cometh from the Lord, which made heaven and earth.   He will not suffer thy foot to be moved: He that keepeth thee will not slumber: behold, He that keepeth Israel shall neither slumber nor sleep.

Unto Thee lift I up mine eyes, O Thou that dwellest in the heavens! Behold, as the eyes of servants look unto the hand of their masters, and as the eyes of a maiden unto the hand of her mistress; so our eyes wait upon the Lord our God, until that He have mercy upon us.

Blessed is the man whom Thou choosest, and causest to approach unto Thee, that he may dwell in Thy courts: we shall be satisfied with the goodness of Thy house, even of Thy holy temple.

Behold, bless ye the Lord, all ye servants of the Lord, which by night stand in the house of the Lord: lift up your hands in the sanctuary, and bless the Lord. The Lord, that made heaven and earth, bless thee out of Zion.

Then follows the singing of a PSALM *or* HYMN *of Praise or Thanksgiving.*

Next the READING OF SCRIPTURE *out of the Old and New Testaments.*

After which the GENERAL PRAYER, *which may be extemporaneous, or else selected from the following forms.*

I.

Almighty God, Most Merciful Father! We do not present ourselves before Thy Majesty trusting in our own merits or worthiness, but in Thy manifold mercies. Thou hast promised to hear our prayers and to grant our requests, in the Name of Thy beloved Son Jesus Christ our Lord: Who also hath commanded us to assemble in His Name, with full assurance that He will be with us, and, as our Mediator and Advocate, obtain all things expedient for our good. Therefore we beseech Thee, Most Merciful Father! turn Thy loving countenance toward us; impute not unto us our manifold offences, whereby we justly deserve Thy wrath; but rather receive us to Thy mercy for Jesus Christ's sake. Accept His death and passion for all our trespasses. In Him alone Thou art well-pleased; and through Him Thou canst not be offended with us. And having of Thy compassion chosen us to be heirs with Him of that immortal Kingdom prepared for us before the foundation of the world: We beseech Thee to increase our faith and knowledge, and to lighten our hearts with Thine Holy Spirit; that we may live in godly conversation, and integrity of life.

And because Thou hast bidden us pray for one another, we make request, O Lord! not only for ourselves, and others whom Thou hast called to the apprehension of Thy will, but for all people and nations of the world. As they know by Thy wonderful works that Thou art God over all, so by Thy Holy Spirit may they learn to believe in Christ, their only Saviour and

Redeemer. But since they can not believe except they hear, nor hear but by preaching, and none can preach except they be sent: Raise up, O Lord! faithful distributors of Thy Mysteries, who, setting aside all worldly considerations, may both in their life and in their doctrine seek only Thy glory. Maintain Thy cause against all opposition ; and strengthen all Thy servants: let not our sins and wickedness prove a hindrance to the spread of Thy Truth; but speedily, O Lord! regard the afflictions of Thy Church; and make haste to save us. Arise, O Lord! and let Thine enemies be ashamed; let them flee from Thy presence that hate Thy holy Name; let the groans of the prisoners come up before Thee ; and preserve by Thy power such as are appointed to die. Let not Thine enemies triumph to the end; but let them understand that against Thee they fight; behold and defend the vine that Thy right hand hath planted; and let all nations see the glory of Thine Anointed. Let Thy mighty hand and outstretched arm be ever our defence; Thy mercy and loving-kindness in Christ our salvation; Thy true and holy Word our instruction; Thy grace and Holy Spirit our consolation, unto the end. Grant these our requests, O Father! and all other things needful for us and Thy whole Church; according to Thy promise in Jesus Christ our Lord: In whose Name we beseech Thee as He hath taught us, saying: OUR FATHER, etc.   KNOX.

II.

Almighty God, our Heavenly Father! We invoke Thy Name, and beseech Thee to turn away Thy face from our manifold sins and transgressions, whereby we have not ceased to draw Thine anger upon us. And because we are most unworthy to appear before Thy sovereign Majesty, be pleased to regard us only in Thy well-beloved Son Jesus Christ; accepting the merits of his death in satisfaction for all our offences, that by His atonement we may become well-pleasing in Thy sight. Pour upon us Thy Holy Spirit, illuminating our minds in the true understanding of Thy Word; and bestow upon us grace, that receiving Thy Truth into our hearts with humility and fear, we may be led to put all our trust in Thee only, and live in Thy service and worship, to the glory of Thy holy Name. These benefits we ask, not only for ourselves, but also for all people and nations on the earth. Bring back, O Lord, into the right way of salvation, all poor captives of ignorance and false doctrine. Raise up true and faithful ministers of the Word, who shall seek not their own ease and ambition, but the exaltation of Thy Name and the safety of Thy flock. Remove and destroy all sects, heresies, and errors, which are the nurseries of strife and dissension in Thy Church; and may all Thy people be of one mind, and live in brotherly union. Rule Thou and govern with Thy Spirit all kings, princes, and magistrates, who hold the administration of the sword; that their dominion be exercised not in avarice, cruelty, and oppression, or any other evil and inordinate affection, but in all justice and uprightness. May we also, living under them, pay them due honour and reverence, and lead quiet and peaceable lives, in all godliness and honesty. Comfort all distressed and afflicted persons, whom Thou dost visit with any kind of cross or tribulation; the nations whom Thou dost chasten with war, pestilence, famine, or any other plague; and all men whom Thou dost afflict with poverty, imprisonment, sickness, banishment, or any other distress of body or infirmity of mind. Give them firm patience under their trials, and speedily bring them out of their afflictions. Confirm and strengthen all Thy faithful children, who in any place are suffering persecution for the testimony of Thy heavenly Truth. Give them stedfast constancy; console them; suffer not the rage of rapacious wolves to prevail against them; but enable them to glorify Thy Name, as well in life as in death. Preserve and defend all Thy Churches which at this day are labouring and fighting for the testimony of Thy blessed Name. Defeat and overturn all the counsels of their enemies, their machinations and devices. So may Thy glory be revealed, and the Kingdom of our Lord Jesus Christ more and more increased and promoted. All this we ask of Thee, as our Sovereign Lord and Master hath taught us to pray: OUR FATHER, etc.

CALVIN.

III.

(Paraphrased upon the Lord's Prayer.)

Our Father which art in heaven! We draw near to Thee with assured confidence through Thy beloved Son; earnestly beseeching that Thy great and holy Name be glorified in every place. Extend Thy dominion over all the earth: leading Thy people by the sceptre of Thy Word, and the power of Thy Spirit: and confounding all Thine enemies by the might of Thy justice and Thy truth. Be pleased to rule over and conduct us; that we may daily learn more and more to submit ourselves to Thy Majesty, as our Governor and King. Destroy every power and principality opposed to Thy glory, until Thy Kingdom be perfectly established, and Thou appear for judgment in the person of Thy Son. Great God! make us able and willing to render Thee true and perfect obedience on earth, as do Thy heavenly angels, that seek only to execute Thy commands. Thus may Thy will without contradiction be fulfilled; and all men submit to Thee, renouncing their own purposes, and all the affections of the flesh.

Grant also, good Lord! that we, walking in the fear and love of Thy holy Name, may through Thy goodness be nourished day by day; and receive at Thy hands all things expedient and necessary for us, that we may use Thy gifts in quietness and peace. And observing Thy care of us, may we better acknowledge Thee to be our Father, expect all benefits at Thy hands only; and withdrawing our confidence from creatures, place it wholly in Thy favour and Thy love.

And because in this mortal life we are so feeble, so sinful, so prone to wander from the right way, and do so continually come short of our duty: We beseech Thee, Lord! forgive our faults, by which we have deserved Thy chastisement; deliver us from that everlasting death unto which we are justly exposed; impute not unto us the evil that dwells within us; and even so may we, according to Thy command, forgive the trespasses of others against us, and do good unto our enemies, rather than seek their hurt.

Finally, O Lord! be pleased to uphold us henceforth by Thy power, lest we fall through the weakness of the flesh. And since of ourselves we are frail, and beset with foes, the world, the flesh, and the devil, that cease not to war against us: Be pleased to fortify us with Thy Spirit, and arm us with Thy grace; may we withstand all manner of temptation, and gain full victory in our spiritual warfare; so that at last we may triumph eternally in Thy Kingdom, with our Sovereign Head and Captain Jesus Christ Thy Son. Amen.

CALVIN.

IV.

O God the Father of Heaven, have mercy upon us.

O God the Son, Redeemer of the world, have mercy upon us.

O God the Holy Ghost, have mercy upon us.

Be merciful unto us and spare us, O Lord.

Be merciful unto us and deliver us, O Lord.

From all sin, from all error, from all evil, from the wiles of the devil, deliver us, O Lord.

From dying suddenly and unprepared; from pestilence and famine, from war and slaughter, from sedition and conspiracy, from lightning and tempest, from everlasting death, deliver us, O Lord.

By the mystery of Thy holy Incarnation, by Thy holy Nativity, by Thy Baptism, Fasting, and Temptations, deliver us, O Lord.

By Thine Agony and bloody Sweat, by Thy Cross and Passion, by Thy Death and Burial, by Thy Resurrection and Ascension, by the coming of the Holy Ghost the Comforter: deliver us, O Lord.

In all time of our tribulation, in all time of our felicity, in the hour of death, in the day of judgment: deliver us, O Lord.

We sinners beseech Thee to hear us.

That it may please Thee to rule and govern Thy holy Church Universal.

That it may please Thee to preserve in soundness of word and holiness of life, all pastors and ministers of Thy Church.

That it may please Thee to remove all sects and scandals.

That it may please Thee to bring back into the way of truth all such as wander and have been led astray.

That it may please Thee to crush Satan under our feet.

That it may please Thee to send forth faithful labourers into Thy harvest.

That it may please Thee to grant the increase of Thy Word and the fruit of Thy Spirit unto all that hear.

That it may please Thee to raise the fallen, and strengthen those that stand.

That it may please Thee to console the weak-hearted, and succour the tempted.

That it may please Thee to give peace and concord unto all rulers and governors.

That it may please Thee to guide and protect our chief magistrate with all his councillors.

That it may please Thee to bless and preserve our people, and all in authority among us.

That it may please Thee to look upon the afflicted, and those that are in danger; and to comfort them.

That it may please Thee to succour all women in the perils of child-birth.

That it may please Thee to cherish and protect young children, and sick persons.

That it may please Thee to defend and suitably provide for the orphans and widows.

That it may please Thee to grant freedom unto captives.

That it may please Thee to have mercy upon all men.

That it may please Thee to forgive our enemies, persecutors, and slanderers, and to convert them.

That it may please Thee to give and preserve the fruits of the earth.

That it may please Thee to grant all these our requests.

We beseech Thee to hear us.

Lamb of God, who takest away the sins of the world, have mercy upon us.

Lamb of God, who takest away the sins of the world, grant us peace.

Lord, deal not with us according to our sins, neither reward us according to our iniquities.

O God, Merciful Father, who despisest not the groans of the contrite, nor rejectest the desire of the sorrowful: Be favourable to our prayers, which, in our afflictions that continually oppress us, we pour out before Thee; and graciously hear them; that those things which the craft of the devil or of man worketh against us, may be brought to nought, and by the counsel of Thy goodness be scattered; that being hurt by no persecutions, we may ever give thanks unto Thee in Thy holy Church: Through Jesus Christ our Lord.

O God, from whom all holy desires, all good counsels, and all just works proceed: Give unto Thy servants that peace which the world can not give; that both our hearts may be set to obey Thy commandments, and also that we, being defended from the fear of our enemies, may by Thy protection pass our time in rest and quietness: Through Jesus Christ our Lord. BUCER.

Our Father which art in heaven, Hallowed be Thy name. Thy kingdom come. Thy will be done in earth, as it is in heaven. Give us this day our daily bread. And forgive us our debts, as we forgive our debtors. And lead us not into temptation, but deliver us from evil: For Thine is the kingdom, and the power, and the glory, for ever. Amen.

After this Prayer a Hymn shall be sung before the

SERMON.

After which another Hymn; and then the

CLOSING PRAYER.

I.

We most humbly beseech Thee, O Father of Mercy, for Jesus Christ Thy Son's sake, that as Thou hast caused the light of Thy Word clearly to shine among us, and hast plainly instructed us by the external Ministry in the right way of salvation: So it may please Thee inwardly to move our dull hearts; and by the power of Thy Holy Spirit to write and seal in them that holy fear and reverence which Thou requirest of Thy chosen. Grant us faithful obedience to Thy holy will, together with the sense that our sins are fully purged and freely remitted, by that One Sacrifice which alone is acceptable to Thee; the obedience, death, and mediation of Thy Son our sovereign Lord, our only Shepherd and High Priest, Jesus Christ; to Whom with Thee and with the Holy Ghost, be all honour and glory, world without end. Amen.   KNOX.

II.

Almighty God, we humbly beseech Thee that the good seed of Thy Word, now sown among us, may take such deep root, that neither the burning heat of affliction shall cause it to wither, nor the cares of this world shall choke it; but that as seed sown in good ground, it may bring forth fruit to Thy praise. And because for our infirmity we can do nothing without Thy help, and Thou knowest how many and sore temptations surround us: Let Thy strength, O Lord, sustain our weakness; let Thy grace defend us from all assaults of evil; increase our faith, that we may never swerve from Thy commandment; augment in us hope and love; and may no hardness of heart, no hypocrisy, no lusts of the flesh, no enticements of the world, draw our hearts away from Thine obedience. Grant this, O Father, we beseech Thee, for the sake of our Advocate and Redeemer, Jesus Christ. Amen.   KNOX.

III.

O God, who dost instruct us by Thy Holy Scriptures, we beseech Thee by Thy grace to enlighten our minds and cleanse our hearts; that having read, heard, and meditated upon them, we may rightly understand and heartily embrace the things Thou hast revealed therein. Give efficacy to the preaching of the Gospel, that through the operation of the Holy Ghost, this holy seed may be received into our hearts as into good ground; and that we may not only hear Thy Word but keep it, living in conformity with Thy precepts; so that we finally attain everlasting salvation, through Jesus Christ our Lord. Amen.   WALDENSIAN LITURGY.

IV.

O Heavenly Father! Thy Word is perfect, converting the soul; a sure testimony, making wise the simple; enlightening the eyes of the blind; and a powerful mean of salvation for all them that believe. Help us, Thine unworthy servants, whether we teach, or whether we be taught, to learn of Thee. We are blind by nature, wholly incapable of doing any good; and Thou wilt help none but them that are of a broken and contrite heart. We beseech Thee to enlighten our understanding with Thy Holy Spirit, and give us a meek heart, free from all haughtiness and carnal knowledge; that we, hearing Thy

Word, may rightly understand it, and rule our lives accordingly. Be graciously pleased to convert all those who still stray from Thy truth; that we, together with them, may unanimously serve Thee in holiness and righteousness all the days of our life. We ask all things for the sake of Jesus Christ our Lord: To Whom with Thee and the Holy Ghost, be all honour and praise evermore. Amen.

REFORMED DUTCH LITURGY.

Benediction.

The grace of the Lord Jesus Christ, and the love of God, and the communion of the Holy Ghost, be with you all. Amen.

THE

MANNER OF CELEBRATING

THE

Sacrament of the Lord's Supper.

I.

The service may be introduced by the singing of a Sacramental Hymn, followed by these prayers.

The Lord's Prayer.

Our Father which art in Heaven, Hallowed be Thy Name. Thy kingdom come. Thy will be done in earth, as it is in heaven. Give us this day our daily bread. And forgive us our debts, as we forgive our debtors. And lead us not into temptation, but deliver us from evil: For Thine is the kingdom, and the power, and the glory, for ever. Amen.

Invocation.

Most Gracious God! whose well-beloved Son hath once offered up His body and blood upon the Cross for the remission of our sins, and doth vouchsafe them for our meat and drink unto life eternal: Grant us grace, with sincere hearts and fervent desires, to accept this great blessing at Thy hands. May we by lively faith partake of His body and blood, yea, of Himself, true God and man, that only bread from heaven, that giveth life unto our souls. Suffer us no more to live unto ourselves, according to a corrupt and sinful nature; but may He live in us, and lead us to the life that is holy, blessed, and unchangeable for ever. Thus may we be partakers of the new and everlasting Testament, which is the Covenant of grace. And thus assure us of Thy willingness ever to be our gracious

Father; not imputing to us our sins, but as Thy beloved heirs and children, providing us with all things needful for our good, that both by our works and words we may magnify Thy Name. Fit us, O heavenly Father! at this time so to celebrate the blessed remembrance of Thy beloved Son. Enable us profitably to contemplate His love, and shew forth the benfits of His death; That receiving fresh increase of strength in Thy faith and in all good works, we may with more confidence call Thee our Father, and evermore rejoice in Thee: Through Jesus Christ our Redeemer. Amen.

Let us now make profession of our faith in the doctrine of the Christian religion, wherein we do all purpose, by the grace of God, to live and to die.

The Creed.

I believe in God the Father Almighty, Maker of heaven and earth: and in Jesus Christ His only Son our Lord; who was conceived by the Holy Ghost, born of the Virgin Mary, suffered under Pontius Pilate, was crucified, dead, and buried; He descended into hell; the third day He rose again from the dead; He ascended into heaven, and sitteth on the right hand of God the Father Almighty; from thence He shall come to judge the quick and the dead. I believe in the Holy Ghost; the Holy Catholic Church, the Communion of Saints; the forgiveness of sins; the resurrection of the body; and the life everlasting. Amen.

Then follows the Exhortation; prefaced with the words of the institution, from 1 Corinthians, xi. 23–30.

Exhortation.

Attend to the words of the institution of the Holy Supper of our Lord Jesus Christ, as they are delivered by the Apostle Paul.

For I have received of the Lord that which also I delivered unto you, That the Lord Jesus, the same night in which He was betrayed, took bread: and when He had given thanks, He brake it, and said, Take, eat; this is my body, which is broken for you: this do in remembrance of me. After the same manner also, He took the cup, when He had supped, saying, This cup is the new testament in my blood: this do ye, as oft as ye drink it, in remembrance of me. For as often as ye eat this bread, and drink this cup, ye do shew the Lord's death till He come. Wherefore, whosoever shall eat this bread, and drink this cup of the Lord, unworthily, shall be guilty of the body and blood of the Lord. But let a man examine himself, and so let him eat of that bread, and drink of that cup. For he that eateth and drinketh unworthily, eateth and drinketh damnation to himself, not discerning the Lord's body.

We have heard, brethren, in what manner our Lord celebrated the Supper among His disciples; whence we see that those who are not of the company of the faithful, may not approach it. Wherefore, in obedience to this rule, in the Name and by the authority of our Lord Jesus Christ, I warn all idolaters, blasphemers, despisers of God, heretics, all that are rebellious against fathers and mothers, all that are seditious, contentious, injurious, and all that lead corrupt and wicked lives: that they abstain from this Table, lest they pollute the sacred food which our Lord giveth only to His faithful servants. Let each of you then, according to St. Paul's exhortation, examine and prove his own conscience, to know whether he have true repentance, and sorrow for his sins; whether he desires henceforth to lead a holy and godly life; above all things, whether he puts his whole trust in God's mercy, and seeks his whole salvation in Jesus Christ; and renouncing all enmity and malice, doth truly and honestly purpose to live in harmony and brotherly love with his neighbour.

If we have this testimony in our hearts before God, we may not doubt that He adopts us for His children, and that our Lord Jesus addresseth to us His word, admitting us to His Table, and presenting us with this holy Sacrament, which He bestows upon His followers. And notwithstanding that we feel many infirmities and miseries in ourselves, as namely, that we have not perfect faith, and that we have not given ourselves to serve God with such zeal as we are bound to do, but have daily to battle with the lusts of our flesh: Yet since the Lord hath been graciously pleased to print His Gospel upon our hearts, and hath enabled us to withstand all unbelief; and hath given us this earnest desire to renounce our own thoughts and follow His righteousness and His holy commandments: Therefore we rest assured, that remaining sins and imperfections do not prevent us from being received of God, and made worthy partakers of this spiritual food. For we come not to this Supper to testify hereby that we are perfect and righteous in ourselves: but on the contrary, seeking our life in Jesus Christ, we acknowledge that we lie in the midst of death. Let us then look upon this Sacrament as a medicine for those who are spiritually sick; and consider that all the worthiness our Lord requires, is that we truly know ourselves, be sorry for our sins, and find our pleasure, joy, and satisfaction in Him above.

First, then, we must believe these promises that Jesus Christ,

3

who is Infallible Truth, hath pronounced with His own lips: That He is truly willing to make us partakers of His body and of His blood, in order that we may wholly possess Him, that He may live in us, and we in Him. And although we see here only the Bread and Wine, let us not doubt that He will accomplish spiritually in our souls all that He outwardly exhibits by these visible signs: He will shew Himself to be the heavenly Bread, to feed and nourish us unto life eternal. Let us not be unthankful to the infinite goodness of our Lord, who displays all His riches at this Table, to distribute them among us. For in giving Himself to us, He testifies that all He hath is ours. Also let us receive this Sacrament as a pledge, that the virtue of His death and passion is imputed unto us for righteousness; even as though we had suffered in our own persons. Let no man perversely draw back, when Jesus doth gently invite him by His Word. But considering the dignity of His precious gift, let us present ourselves to Him with an ardent zeal, that He may make us capable of receiving it.

And now to this end lift up your minds and hearts on high, where Christ abideth in the glory of His Father, whence we expect His coming at our redemption. Dwell not on these earthly and corruptible elements, which we see present to our eyes, and feel with our hands, to seek Him in them, as though He were inclosed in the bread or in the wine. Be satisfied to have this bread and this wine for witnesses and signs; seeking spiritually the truth where God's Word hath promised that we shall find it. For then only shall our souls be disposed to receive food and life from His substance, when they shall thus be lifted above all worldly things, even unto heaven, and enter into the kingdom of God, where He dwells.

The Consecrating Prayer.

Lord God! The Father of our Lord Jesus Christ! Thou that art infinite goodness and perfect love! We bring Thee the sacrifice of our praise and the offering up of our thanks, for Thine inestimable gift in sending Thy Son into the world; for delivering Him up to die for us all; and for inviting us to participate in the fruits of His atonement, at the Table of this holy feast. Lord! what are we, to receive such priceless benefits at Thy hand? or how shall we worthily shew forth our gratitude to Thee? The heavens and the earth, O Lord! are full of the tokens of Thy bounty: but especially dost Thou manifest Thy love, in that while we were yet sinners, Christ died for us. Accept, O Lord our God! the homage of Thine adoring people. And grant that we, partaking of this holy Sacrament, to which we are welcomed by Thy grace, may now join ourselves by the bonds of living faith and true holiness to our Saviour: so that we shall not henceforth live unto ourselves, but that He may live in us, to lead us to that blessed life that shall have no end.

Father of Mercies! who didst not spare Thine only-begotten Son, but deliveredst Him to death for us all; and hast brought us into His fellowship that we may obtain everlasting life: We Thy servants, with a lively sense of Thy precious gift, do now consecrate ourselves entirely unto Thee. We present to Thee our bodies, and our souls, in a living and holy sacrifice. And since Thou hast loved us so much, we acknowledge ourselves constrained to love one another. Impress our hearts, O God! with these holy inclinations: that so celebrating the remembrance of Thy dear Son, our faith may grow strong, our charity increase, our sanctification advance and be made complete, until we be meet for the inheritance of Thy saints in light everlasting. Hear us, O Father of Mercies! we ask all in the Name of Thy well-beloved Son Jesus Christ our Lord: unto Whom, as unto Thee, and the Holy Ghost, one God, be honour, praise, and glory, now, henceforth, and for ever. Amen.

Then the Minister is to take the Bread and break it, in the view of the people, saying:

Our Lord Jesus Christ, on the same night in which He was betrayed, having taken bread, and blessed and broken it, gave it to His disciples; as I, ministering in His Name, give this bread unto you: saying, [*here the bread is to be distributed,*] Take, eat: this is My body, which is broken for you: this do in remembrance of Me.

After having given the Bread, he shall take the Cup, and say.

After the same manner our Saviour also took the cup; and having given thanks, as hath been done in His Name, He gave it to the disciples; saying, [*here the cup is to be given,*] This cup is the new testament in My blood, which is shed for many, for the remission of sins: drink ye all of it. For as often as ye eat this bread, and drink this cup, ye do shew the Lord's death till He come.

The Minister himself is to communicate, at such time as may appear to him most convenient.

Then let an eucharistic hymn be sung.

The collection for the poor may be made after this

Then the Minister is to pray, and give thanks to God.

Thanksgiving.

Heavenly Father! we give Thee immortal praise and thanks that upon us poor sinners Thou hast conferred so rich a benefit, as to bring us into the communion of Thy Son Jesus Christ our Lord. Him having delivered up to death for us, Thou hast given for our food and nourishment unto eternal life. Now also grant us grace, that we may never be unmindful of these things; but carrying them about engraven on our hearts, may we advance and grow in that faith which is effectual unto every good work. Thus may the rest of our lives be ordered and followed out to Thy glory and the good of our fellow-men: Through Jesus Christ our Lord: Who with Thee, O Father! and the Holy Ghost, liveth and reigneth in the unity of the Godhead, world without end. Amen.

Benediction.

Now the God of Peace, that brought again from the dead our Lord Jesus, that great Shepherd of the sheep, through the blood of the everlasting covenant, make you perfect in every good work to do His will, working in you that which is well-pleasing in His sight, through Jesus Christ; to Whom be glory for ever and ever. Amen.

> [From CALVIN, with the exceptions of the Consecrating Prayer from the Liturgy of Geneva; and the Manner of setting apart the Elements, from the Directory of Worship.]

II.

The service may begin with the singing of a hymn, followed by the Lord's Prayer, Invocation, and Creed, as in the first Form.

Exhortation.

Let us mark, dear brethren, how Jesus Christ did ordain unto us His Holy Supper, according as St. Paul maketh rehearsal in the eleventh chapter of the First Epistle to the Corinthians, saying:

For I have received of the Lord that which also I delivered unto you, That the Lord Jesus, the same night in which He was betrayed, took bread: and when He had given thanks, He brake it, and said, Take, eat; this is my body, which is broken for you: this do in remembrance of me. After the same manner also, He took the cup, when He had supped, saying, This cup is the new testament in my blood: this do ye, as oft as ye drink it, in remembrance of me. For as often as ye eat this bread, and drink this cup, ye do shew the Lord's death till He come. Wherefore, whosoever shall eat this bread, and drink this cup of the Lord, unworthily, shall be guilty of the body and blood of the Lord. But let a man examine himself, and so let him eat of that bread, and drink of that cup. For he that eateth and drinketh unworthily, eateth and drinketh damnation to himself, not discerning the Lord's body.

Dearly beloved in the Lord, forasmuch as we are now assembled to celebrate the holy Communion of the body and blood of our Saviour Christ, let us consider these words of St. Paul, how he exhorteth all persons diligently to try and examine themselves, before they presume to eat of that bread, and to drink of that cup. For as the benefit is great, if with a true penitent heart and lively faith we receive that holy sacrament, for then we spiritually eat the flesh of Christ, and drink His blood; then we dwell in Christ, and Christ in us; we be one with Christ, and Christ with us:—So is the danger great if we receive the same unworthily; for then we be guilty of the body and blood of Christ our Saviour; we eat and drink our own condemnation, not discerning the Lord's body; we kindle God's wrath against us, and provoke His punishment upon us.

And therefore, in the Name and by the authority of the Eternal God, and of His Son Jesus Christ, I separate from this Table all blasphemers of God, all idolaters, all that be in malice or envy, all persons disobedient to father or mother, and finally all such as live a life directly fighting against the will of God: charging them, as they will answer in the presence of Him who is the righteous Judge, that they presume not to profane this most holy Table.

And yet this I pronounce not to exclude any penitent person, how grievous soever his sins before have been, so that he feel in his heart unfeigned repentance for the same : but only such as continue in sin without repentance. Neither yet is this pronounced against such as aspire to a greater perfection than they can in this present life attain. For albeit we feel in ourselves much frailty and wretchedness, so that we have not faith so perfect and constant as we ought, being many times ready to distrust God's goodness, through our corrupt nature ; and also that we are not so thoroughly given to serve God, neither have so fervent a zeal to set forth His glory as our duty requireth ; feeling still such rebellion in ourselves, that we have need daily to fight against the lusts of our flesh :—Yet nevertheless seeing that our Lord hath dealt thus mercifully with us, that He hath printed His Gospel in our hearts, so that we are preserved from falling into despair and unbelief; and seeing that He hath endued us with a will and desire to renounce and

withstand our own affections, with a longing for His righteousness and the keeping of His commandments: We may be now
right well assured, that these failures and manifold imperfections
shall be no such hindrance against us, as that He should not
accept us, and count us worthy to come to His spiritual Table.
For the end of our coming is not to protest that we are just
and upright in our lives; but contrariwise, we come to seek our
life and perfection in Jesus Christ; acknowledging in the meantime that we of ourselves are children of wrath and condemnation.

Let us then consider this Sacrament as a precious medicine
for all poor sick creatures, a comfortable help to weak souls;
and that our Lord requireth no other worthiness on our part,
than this: that we unfeignedly acknowledge our sinfulness and
imperfection. Then to the end that we may be worthy partakers of His merits and most comfortable benefits, which is
the true eating of His flesh and drinking of His blood, let us
not suffer our minds to wander about the consideration of these
earthly and corruptible things, which we see present to our
eyes and feel with our hands; to seek Christ bodily present in
them, as if He were enclosed in the bread and wine, or as if
these elements were turned and changed into the substance of
His flesh and blood. But as the only way to dispose our
souls to receive nourishment, relief, and quickening of His
substance, let us lift up our minds by faith above all things
worldly and sensible, and thereby enter into heaven, that we
may find and receive Christ where He dwelleth undoubtedly,
very God and very man, in the incomprehensible glory of His
Father: to Whom be all praise, honour, and glory, now and
ever. Amen.

The Consecrating Prayer.

O Father of Mercy, and God of all consolation! Thou
whom all creatures acknowledge and confess as Governor and
Lord: It becomes us, the workmanship of Thine hands, at all
times to reverence and magnify Thy holy Majesty; For that
Thou hast created us in Thine image; but chiefly that Thou
hast delivered us from everlasting death and condemnation,
whereunto we were drawn by means of sin: from the bondage
whereof neither man nor angel was able to make us free. And
we do praise Thee, O Lord! that rich in mercy and infinite in
goodness, Thou hast provided our redemption to stand in Thine
only and well-beloved Son: Whom of very love Thou didst
give to be made man like unto us in all things, sin excepted;
in His body to receive the punishment of our transgression;
by His death to make satisfaction to Thy justice; and through

His resurrection to destroy him that was the author of death, and so to bring again life to the world, from which the whole offspring of Adam most justly was exiled.

O Lord ! we acknowledge that no creature is able to comprehend the length and breadth, the depth and height, of that Thy most excellent love; which moved Thee to shew mercy where none was deserved; to promise and give life where death had gotten the victory; to receive us again in Thy favour, when we could do nothing but rebel against Thy law. O Lord! the blind dulness of our corrupt nature will not suffer us sufficiently to weigh these Thy most ample benefits. Yet nevertheless, at the command of Jesus Christ our Lord, we present ourselves at this His Table, which He hath left to be used in remembrance of His death, until His coming again: to dedicate ourselves unto His service, renewing our vows, and engaging henceforth to obey His will; to declare and witness before the world, that by Him alone Thou dost acknowledge us Thy children; that by Him alone we have access to Thy throne of grace; that by Him alone we are brought into His spiritual Kingdom, to eat and drink at His Table; with whom we have our conversation even now in heaven; and by whom our bodies shall be raised up again from the dust, and shall be placed with Him in that endless joy, which Thou, O Father of Mercy! hadst prepared for Thine elect before the foundation of the world was laid. And these most inestimable benefits, we acknowledge to have received of Thy free mercy and grace, by Thine only-begotten Son Jesus Christ our Lord: for the which therefore we Thy congregation, moved by Thine Holy Spirit, render all thanks, praise, and glory, for ever and ever. Amen.

Then the Minister is to take the Bread, and break it, in the view of the people, saying :

Our Lord Jesus Christ, on the same night in which He was betrayed, having taken bread, and blessed and broken it, gave it to His disciples; as I, ministering in His Name, give this bread unto you: saying, [*here the bread is to be distributed,*] Take, eat; this is My body, which is broken for you: this do in remembrance of Me.

After having given the Bread, he shall take the Cup, and say :

After the same manner our Saviour also took the cup; and having given thanks, as hath been done in His Name, He gave it to the disciples; saying, [*here the cup is to be given,*] This cup is the new testament in My blood, which is shed for many, for the remission of sins: drink ye all of it. For as often as ye eat this bread, and drink this cup, ye do shew the Lord's death till He come.

The Minister himself is to communicate, at such time as may appear to him most convenient.

Then let an eucharistic hymn be sung.

The collection for the poor may be made after this.

Then the Minister is to pray, and give thanks to God.

Thanksgiving.

Most Merciful Father! we render Thee all praise, thanks, and glory, for that it hath pleased Thee, of Thy great mercies, to grant us miserable sinners so excellent a gift, as to receive us into the fellowship and company of Thy dear Son Jesus Christ our Lord; whom Thou hast delivered to death for us, and given as our needful food and nourishment unto everlasting life. And now we beseech Thee also, Heavenly Father! to grant our prayer, that Thou wilt never suffer us to forget these worthy benefits; but rather imprint and fasten them surely in our hearts, that we may grow and increase daily more and more in that true faith, which is continually exercised in all manner of good works. Confirm us, O Lord! that we may stand immoveable in the profession of Thy Name, to the advancement of Thy glory, who art God over all things, blessed for ever. So be it. Amen.

Benediction.

Now the God of Peace, that brought again from the dead our Lord Jesus, that great Shepherd of the sheep, through the blood of the everlasting covenant, make you perfect in every good work to do His will, working in you that which is well-pleasing in His sight, through Jesus Christ; to Whom be glory for ever and ever. Amen.   KNOX.

III.

The service may begin with the singing of a Hymn, followed by the Lord's Prayer, Invocation, and Creed, as in the first Form.

Exhortation.

Hear what the Apostle Paul saith: For I have received of the Lord that which also I delivered unto you, That the Lord Jesus, the same night in which He was betrayed, took bread:

and when He had given thanks, He brake it, and said, Take, eat; this is my body, which is broken for you: this do in remembrance of me. After the same manner also, He took the cup, when He had supped, saying, This cup is the new testament in my blood: this do ye, as oft as ye drink it, in remembrance of me. For as often as ye eat this bread, and drink this cup, ye do shew the Lord's death till He come. Wherefore, whosoever shall eat this bread, and drink this cup of the Lord, unworthily, shall be guilty of the body and blood of the Lord. But let a man examine himself, and so let him eat of that bread, and drink of that cup. For he that eateth and drinketh unworthily, eateth and drinketh damnation to himself, not discerning the Lord's body.

You are invited hither, dear brethren, to be guests at this holy Table, by the Lord's command, to receive the greatest mercy, and to perform the greatest duty. On Christ's part all things are made ready. The feast is prepared for you, even for you that by sin have deserved to be cast out of the presence of the Lord; for you that have so oft neglected and abused mercy: a feast of the body and blood of Christ, free to you, but dear to Him. You were lost, and in the way to be lost for ever; when by the greatest miracle of condescending love, He sought and saved you. You were dead in sin, condemned by the law, the slaves of Satan; there wanted nothing but the executing stroke of justice to have sent you into endless misery: when our Redeemer pitied you in your blood, and shed His own to wash and heal you. He suffered who was offended, that the offender might not suffer. He cried out on the cross, My God, my God, why hast thou forsaken me? that we, who had deserved it, might not be everlastingly forsaken. He died, that we might live. O, how should this mercy of redemption affect you! See here Christ dying in this holy representation! Behold the sacrificed Lamb of God, that taketh away the sins of the world. It is His will to be thus frequently crucified before our eyes. O, how should we be covered with shame, and loathe ourselves, who have both procured the death of Christ by sin, and sinned against it. And how should we all be filled with joy, who have such mysteries of mercy opened, and so great salvation freely offered to us. O, hate sin. O, love this Saviour. See that you come not hither without a desire to be more holy; nor with a purpose to go on in wilful sin. Be not deceived, God is not mocked. But if you heartily repent, and consent to the covenant, come, and welcome. We have commission from Christ to tell you that you are welcome. Let no trembling, contrite soul draw back, that is willing to be Christ's upon His covenant terms: but believe that Christ is much more willing to be yours. He was first willing, and therefore died for you, and made the covenant of grace, and sent to invite and importune you to consent, and stayed for you so long, and gave you your repentance, your willingness, and desire. Question not then His willingness, if you are willing: it is Satan and unbelief that would have you question it, to the injury both of Christ and you. Come near, observe, believe, and wonder at the riches of His love and grace: for He hath Himself invited you to see and taste, that you might wonder. You are sinners: but He inviteth you to receive a renewed, sealed pardon of your sins, and to give you more of His Spirit to overcome them. See here His broken body and His blood, the testimonies of His willingness. Thus hath He sealed the covenant, which pardoneth all your sins, and secureth you of your reconciliation with God, and your adoption, and your right to everlasting blessedness. Deny not your consent, but heartily give up yourselves to Christ: and then doubt not that your scarlet, crimson sins shall be made as white as wool or snow. Object not the number or greatness of them against His grace: there is none too great for Him to pardon to penitent believers. But strive you then for great loathing of your sins, and greater love to such a God, aad greater thanks to such a Saviour. Unfeignedly say, I am willing, Lord, to be wholly Thine: and then believingly take Christ, and pardon, and life, as given you by His own appointment in the sealed covenant. And remember that He is coming. He is coming with thousands of His mighty angels, to execute judgment on the ungodly; but to be glorified in His saints, and admired in all that do believe. And then we shall have greater things than these. Then shall you see all the promises fulfilled, which now are sealed to you, on which He causeth you to trust. Revive now your love to one another, and forgive those that have wronged you, and delight in the communion of saints: and then you shall be admitted into the Church triumphant, where, with perfect saints, you shall perfectly rejoice, and love and praise the Lord forever. Receive now a crucified Christ here represented, and be content to take up your cross, and follow Him. And then you shall reign with a glorified Christ, in the blessed vision and fruition of that God, to whom by Christ you are now reconciled. Let faith and love be working upon these things, while you are at this holy Table.

The Consecrating Prayer.

Almighty God, Thou art the Creator and the Lord of all things. Thou art the sovereign Majesty whom we have offended. Thou art our most loving and merciful Father, who hast given Thy Son to reconcile us to Thyself: who hath ratified the new testament and covenant of grace with His most precious blood; and hath instituted this holy Sacrament to be celebrated in remembrance of Him till His coming. Sanctify these Thy creatures of bread and wine, which according to Thy institution and command we set apart to this holy use, that they may be sacramentally the body and blood of Thy Son Jesus Christ.

Most merciful Saviour, as Thou hast loved us to the death, and suffered for our sins, the just for the unjust, and hast instituted this holy ordinance to be used in remembrance of Thee till Thy coming: We beseech Thee, by Thine intercession with the Father, through the sacrifice of Thy body and blood, give us the pardon of our sins, and Thy quickening Spirit, without which the flesh will profit us nothing. Reconcile us to the Father; nourish us as Thy members to everlasting life.

Most Holy Spirit, proceeding from the Father and the Son; by whom Christ was conceived; by whom the prophets and apostles were inspired, and the ministers of Christ are qualified and called; Thou that dwellest and workest in all the members of Christ, whom Thou sanctifiest to the image and for the service of their Head, and comfortest that they may show forth His praise: Illuminate us, that by faith we may see Him who is here represented to us. Soften our hearts, and humble us for our sins. Sanctify and quicken us, that we may relish the spiritual food, and feed on it to our nourishment and growth in grace. Shed abroad the love of God upon our hearts, and draw them out in love to Him. Fill us with thankfulness and holy joy, and with love to one another. Comfort us by witnessing that we are the children of God. Confirm us for new obedience. Be the earnest of our inheritance, and seal us unto everlasting life.

Accept us, O Lord! who resign ourselves unto Thee as Thine own; and with our thanks and praise, present ourselves a living sacrifice, to be acceptable through Christ, useful for Thine honour, through time, and through eternity. Being made free from sin, and become Thy servants, let us have our fruit unto holiness, and the end everlasting life: Through Jesus Christ our Lord and Saviour. Amen.

Then the Minister is to take the Bread, and break it, in the view of the people, saying:

Our Lord Jesus Christ, on the same night in which He was betrayed, having taken bread, and blessed and broken it, gave it to His disciples; as I, ministering in His Name, give this

bread unto you: saying, [*here the bread is to be distributed,*] Take,
eat: this is My body, which is broken for you: this do in remembrance of Me.

After having given the Bread, let him take the Cup, and say:

After the same manner our Saviour also took the cup, and
having given thanks, as hath been done in His Name, He gave
it to the disciples; saying, [*here the cup is to be given,*] This cup
is the new testament in My blood, which is shed for many, for
the remission of sins: drink ye all of it. For as often as ye
eat this bread, and drink this cup, ye do shew the Lord's death
till he come.

*The Minister himself is to communicate, at such time as may appear to him most
convenient.*

Then let an eucharistic hymn be sung.

The Collection for the poor may be made after this.

Then the Minister is to pray, and give thanks to God.

Thanksgiving.

Most Glorious God, how wonderful Thy power and wisdom, Thy holiness and justice, Thy love and mercy, in this
work of redemption, by the incarnation, life, death, resurrection, intercession, and dominion of Thy Son! No wisdom or
power in heaven or earth could have delivered us but Thine.
The angels desire to look into this mystery: the heavenly host
do celebrate it with praises, saying, Glory to God in the high-
est: on earth peace, good-will towards men. The whole creation shall proclaim Thy praises: Blessing, honour, glory,
and power, be unto Him that sitteth upon the throne, and
unto the Lamb forever and ever. Worthy is the Lamb that
was slain, to receive power, and honour, and glory: for He
hath redeemed us to God by His blood, and made us kings
and priests unto our God. And hast Thou indeed forgiven us
so great a debt, by so precious a ransom? Wilt Thou indeed give us to reign with Christ in glory, and see Thy face,
and love Thee and be loved of Thee for ever? Yea, Lord!
Thou hast forgiven us, and wilt glorify us; for Thou art faithful that hast promised. O set our affections on the things
above: let our conversation be in heaven, from whence we
expect our Saviour to come and change us into the likeness
of His glory. Then will we perfectly praise and worthily
magnify Thee for ever, O Father, Son, and Holy Ghost: to
whom be glory. Amen.

Benediction.

Now the God of Peace, that brought again from the dead our Lord Jesus, that great Shepherd of the sheep, through the blood of the everlasting covenant, make you perfect in every good work to do His will, working in you that which is well-pleasing in His sight, through Jesus Christ: to Whom be glory for ever and ever. Amen. BAXTER.

IV.

The service may begin with the singing of a hymn, followed by the

Exhortation.

Beloved in the Lord Jesus Christ, attend to the words of the institution of the holy Supper of our Lord Jesus Christ, as they are delivered by the holy Apostle Paul.

For I have received of the Lord that which also I delivered unto you, That the Lord Jesus, the same night in which He was betrayed, took bread: and when He had given thanks, He brake it, and said, Take, eat; this is my body, which is broken for you: this do in remembrance of me. After the same manner also He took the cup, when He had supped, saying, This cup is the new testament in my blood: this do ye, as oft as ye drink it, in remembrance of me. For as often as ye eat this bread, and drink this cup, ye do shew the Lord's death till He come. Wherefore, whosoever shall eat this bread, and drink this cup of the Lord, unworthily, shall be guilty of the body and blood of the Lord. But let a man examine himself, and so let him eat of that bread, and drink of that cup. For he that eateth and drinketh unworthily, eateth and drinketh damnation* to himself, not discerning the Lord's body.

That we may now celebrate the Supper of the Lord to our comfort, it is necessary first that every one consider by himself his sins, and the curse due to him for them: to the end that he may abhor and humble himself before God; considering that the wrath of God against sin is so great, that rather than it should go unpunished, He hath punished the same in His beloved Son Jesus Christ, with the bitter and shameful death of the cross.

Secondly, Let every one examine his own heart, whether he doth believe this faithful promise of God: that all his sins are

---

* Gr.—κριμα. D.—Oordeel. E.—Judgment, condemnation.

forgiven him, only for the sake of the passion and death of Jesus Christ; and that the perfect righteousness of Christ is imputed and freely given to him as his own; yea, so perfectly as if he had in his own person satisfied for all his sins, and fulfilled all righteousness.

Thirdly, Let every one examine his own conscience, whether he hath resolved henceforth to shew true thankfulness to God in his whole life, and to walk uprightly before Him : and also whether he hath laid aside unfeignedly all enmity, hatred, and envy, and doth firmly resolve henceforward to walk in true love and peace with his neighbour.

All those who are thus disposed, God will certainly receive in mercy, and count them worthy partakers at the table of His Son Jesus Christ. On the contrary, those who do not feel this testimony in their hearts, eat and drink judgment to themselves. Therefore, we also, according to the command of Christ and the Apostle Paul, admonish all those who know themselves to be defiled with the following sins, to keep themselves from the Table of the Lord; and declare to them that they have no part of the Kingdom of Christ. Such as are idolaters; all those who use or confide in any form of divination; all despisers of God and of His Word, and of the holy Sacraments; all profane or false swearers; contentious persons, and those who live in hatred and envy against their neighbours; all unclean persons, drunkards, thieves, liars, slanderers, covetous; and all who lead offensive lives. These, while they continue in such sins, shall abstain 'from this meat which Christ hath ordained only for the faithful; lest their judgment and condemnation be made the heavier.

But this is not designed, dearly beloved brethren and sisters in the Lord, to deject the contrite hearts of the faithful; as if none might come to this Supper, but such as are without sin. For we do not come to this Supper to testify thereby that we are perfect and righteous in ourselves: but on the contrary, since we are seeking our life out of ourselves, in Jesus Christ, we acknowledge by this very service that we lie in the midst of death. Therefore, notwithstanding we still find many short-comings and miseries in ourselves; as namely, that we have not perfect faith; and that we do not give ourselves to serve God with that zeal as we are bound; but have daily to strive with the weakness of our faith, and the evil lusts of our own flesh; yet since, by the grace of the Holy Ghost, we are sorry for these weaknesses, and earnestly desirous to fight against our unbelief, and to live according to all the commandments of God : Therefore, we rest assured, that no sin or infirmity which still against our will remaineth in us, can hinder us from being received of God in mercy, and thus made worthy partakers of this heavenly meat and drink.

Let us now also consider to what end the Lord hath instituted His Supper: namely, That ye do it in remembrance of Him. Now after this manner are we to remember Him in it. First, We must be confidently persuaded in our hearts, that our Lord Jesus Christ was sent of the Father into the world; He assumed our flesh and blood; He bore for us the wrath of God, under which we should have perished everlastingly, from the beginning of His incarnation to the end of His life upon earth; especially when the weight of our sins and of the wrath of God pressed out of Him the bloody sweat in the garden, where he was bound that our bonds might be loosed. Afterwards He suffered innumerable revilings, that we might never come to shame. In His innocence He was condemned to death, that we might be acquitted at the judgment-seat of God. Yea, He suffered His blessed body to be nailed on the Cross, that He might fasten thereon that handwriting of our sins. And hath also taken upon Himself the curse due to us, that He might fill us with His blessings; and humbled Himself unto the deepest reproach and pains of hell, in body and in soul, on the tree of the Cross, when He cried with a loud voice, My God, my God, why hast Thou forsaken me: that we might be made nigh unto God, and never be forsaken of Him. And finally He confirmed with His death and the shedding of His blood the new and eternal testament, that covenant of grace and reconciliation; when He said, It is finished. And that we might firmly believe that we belong to this covenant of grace, the Lord Jesus Christ hath ordained this Holy Supper, and said, This do in remembrance of Me: That is, as often as ye eat of this bread and drink of this cup, ye shall thereby, as by a sure memorial and pledge, be admonished and assured of this my hearty love and faithfulness toward you. That whereas you should otherwise have suffered eternal death, I have given my body to the death of the Cross, and have shed my blood for you, and with my crucified body and shed blood do nourish your hungry and thirsty souls to everlasting life, as surely as this bread is broken before your eyes, and this cup is given to you, and you eat and drink the same with your mouth, in remembrance of Me.

From this institution of the Holy Supper of our Lord Jesus Christ, we see that He directs our faith and trust to His perfect sacrifice once offered on the Cross, as to the only ground of our salvation; wherein He is become to our hungry and thirsty souls the true meat and drink of life eternal. For by His

death He hath taken away the cause of our eternal death
and misery; namely, sin: and obtained for us the life-giving
Spirit; that we by the same, which dwelleth in Christ as in
the Head, and in us as in His members, might have true communion with Him, and be made partakers of all His blessings,
of life eternal, righteousness, and glory. And furthermore,
that we by the same Spirit may also be united as members of
one Body in true brotherly love; as the holy Apostle saith,
For we being many are one bread and one body: for we are
all partakers of that one bread. For as out of many grains
one meal is ground and one bread baked; and out of many
berries being pressed together one wine floweth and mixeth
itself together: so all we, who by a true faith are engrafted
into Christ, shall through brotherly love be one body for the
sake of Christ our beloved Saviour, who hath first so exceed-
ingly loved us. And this we shall shew not only in word, but
also in very deed.

Hereto assist us the Almighty God and Father of our Lord
Jesus Christ, through His Holy Spirit. Amen.

That we may obtain all this, let us humble ourselves before
God, and with true faith implore His grace.

The Consecrating Prayer.

O Most Merciful God and Father! we beseech Thee that in
this Supper, by which we celebrate the glorious remembrance
of the bitter death of Thy beloved Son Jesus Christ, Thou
wilt so work in our hearts by Thy Holy Spirit, that with true
confidence we may more and more give ourselves up unto Thy
Son Jesus Christ; that our burthened and fainting hearts may,
through the power of the Holy Ghost, be fed and comforted
with His true body and blood, yea, with Him, true God and
man, that only heavenly Bread. And may we no longer live
in our sins, but He in us and we in Him; and thus be true
partakers of the new and everlasting covenant of grace. May
we not doubt that Thou wilt for ever be our gracious Father,
never more imputing our sins unto us, and providing us as
Thy beloved children and heirs, with all things necessary as
well for the body as tho soul. Grant us also Thy grace, that
we may cheerfully take upon us our cross, deny ourselves, confess our Saviour, and in all tribulations with uplifted heads
expect our Lord Jesus Christ from heaven, where He will make
our mortal bodies like unto His most glorious body, and take
us to be for ever with Himself.

Our Father which art in Heaven, Hallowed be Thy Name.
Thy kingdom come. Thy will be done in earth, as it is in
heaven. Give us this day our daily bread. And forgive us

our debts, as we forgive our debtors. And lead us not into temptation, but deliver us from evil: For Thine is the king-dom, and the power, and the glory, for ever. Amen.

Strengthen us also by this holy Supper in the Catholic un-doubted Christian Faith, whereof we make confession with our mouths and hearts, saying:

I believe in God the Father Almighty, Maker of heaven and earth: and in Jesus Christ His only Son our Lord; who was conceived by the .Holy Ghost, born of the Virgin Mary, suf-fered under Pontius Pilate, was crucified, dead, and buried; He descended into hell; the third day He rose again from the dead; He ascended into heaven, and sitteth on the right hand of God the Father Almighty; from thence He shall come to judge the quick and the dead. I believe in the Holy Ghost; the Holy Catholic Church, the Communion of Saints; the forgiveness of sins; the resurrection of the body, and the life everlasting. Amen.

That we may now be fed with the true heavenly Bread, Christ Jesus, let us not cleave with our hearts unto the external bread and wine, but lift them up on high, where Christ Jesus is our Advocate, at the right hand of His heavenly Father; whither all the articles of our faith lead us: not doubting that through the working of the Holy Ghost, we shall be fed and refreshed in our souls with His body and blood, as surely as we receive the holy bread and wine in remembrance of Him.

Then the Minister is to take the Bread, and break it in the view of the people, saying:

Our Lord Jesus Christ, on the same night in which He was betrayed, having taken bread, and blessed and broken it, gave it to His disciples; as I, ministering in His Name, give this bread unto you: saying, [*here the bread is to be distributed,*] Take, eat; this is My body, which is broken for you: this do in remembrance of Me.

After having given the Bread, he shall take the Cup, and say:

After the same manner our Saviour also took the cup; and having given thanks, as hath been done in His Name, He gave it to the disciples; saying, [*here the cup is to be given,*] This cup is the new testament in My blood, which is shed for many, for the remission of sins: drink ye all of it. For as often as ye eat this bread, and drink this cup, ye do shew the Lord's death till He come.

4

In distributing the Bread, the Minister shall say:

The bread which we break is the communion of the body of Christ.

And when he giveth the Cup:

The cup of blessing which we bless is the communion of the blood of Christ.

During the Communion there shall or may be devoutly sung a Psalm, or some chapter read, in remembrance of the death of Christ: as Isaiah LIII., St. John XIII., XIV., XVI., XVII., XVIII., or the like.

After the Communion, the Minister shall say:

Beloved in the Lord, since the Lord hath now fed our souls at His Table, let us therefore jointly praise His holy Name with thanksgiving, and every one say in his heart thus:

Bless the Lord, O my soul: and all that is within me, bless His holy Name.

Bless the Lord, O my soul: and forget not all His benefits.

Who forgiveth all thine iniquities: who healeth all thy diseases.

Who redeemeth thy life from destruction: who crowneth thee with loving-kindness and tender mercies.

The Lord is merciful and gracious: slow to anger and plenteous in mercy.

He hath not dealt with us after our sins: nor rewarded us according to our iniquities.

For as the heaven is high above the earth: so great is His mercy toward them that fear Him.

As far as the East is from the West: so far hath He removed our transgressions from us.

Like as a Father pitieth his children: so the Lord pitieth them that fear Him.

Who hath not spared His own Son, but delivered Him up for us all, and given us all things with Him. Therefore God commendeth therewith His love towards us, in that while we were yet sinners, Christ died for us. Much more then, being now justified in His blood, we shall be saved from wrath through Him. For if, when we were enemies, we were reconciled to God by the death of His Son: much more being reconciled we shall be saved by His life. Therefore shall my mouth and heart show forth the praises of the Lord from this time for evermore. Amen.

Then let an eucharistic hymn be sung.

The collection for the poor may be made after this.

Then the Minister is to pray, and give thanks to God.

Thanksgiving.

Let every one say with an attentive heart:

O Almighty, Merciful God and Father, with our whole hearts we thank Thee, that Thou hast of Thy boundless mercy given us Thine only-begotten Son, to be our Mediator, and the sacrifice for our sins, and our meat and drink unto life eternal. We bless Thee that Thou givest us lively faith, whereby we are made partakers of such Thy benefits: and hast been pleased that Thy beloved Son Jesus Christ should ordain His holy Supper for the confirmation of the same. Grant then we beseech Thee, O faithful God and Father, that through the working of Thy Holy Spirit, this remembrance made of our Lord Jesus Christ, and this shewing forth of His death, may tend to the daily increase of our faith and saving fellowship with Him: Unto Whom, as unto Thee, O Father! and the Holy Ghost, be honour and praise for ever. Amen.

Benediction.

Now the God of Peace, that brought again from the dead our Lord Jesus, that great Shepherd of the sheep, through the blood of the everlasting covenant, make you perfect in every good work to do His will, working in you that which is well-pleasing in His sight, through Jesus Christ, to whom be glory for ever and ever. Amen. REFORMED DUTCH LITURGY.

SENTENCES,

Which may be repeated by the Minister, at intervals of silence, during the participation.

The Bread which we break, is the communion of the Body of Christ.

I am the Bread of life, saith Jesus: he that cometh to Me shall never hunger; and he that believeth on Me shall never thirst.

The Son of Man came, to give His life a ransom for many.

He was wounded for our transgressions, He was bruised for our iniquities: the chastisement of our peace was upon Him; and with His stripes we are healed.

He was oppressed, and He was afflicted, yet He opened not His mouth.

Surely He hath borne our griefs, and carried our sorrows.

Behold the Lamb of God, which taketh away the sins of the world.

This is a faithful saying, and worthy of all acceptation, that Christ Jesus came into the world to save sinners; of whom I am the chief.

Come unto Him, all ye that labour and are heavy laden, and He will give you rest. Take His yoke upon you, and learn of Him: for He is meek and lowly in heart: and ye shall find rest unto your souls.

And now, little children, abide in Him; that when He shall appear, we may have confidence, and not be ashamed at His coming.

The Cup of Blessing which we bless, is the communion of the Blood of Christ.

I am the Vine, saith Jesus, ye are the branches; abide in Me and I in you.

Greater love hath no man than this, that a man lay down his life for his friends: ye are My friends, if ye do whatsoever I command you.

God so loved the world, that He gave His only-begotten Son, that whosoever believeth in Him should not perish, but have everlasting life.

Hereby perceive we the love of God, because He laid down His life for us: and we ought to lay down our lives for the brethren.

Behold, what manner of love the Father hath bestowed upon us, that we should be called the sons of God.

We know that when He shall appear, we shall be like Him: for we shall see Him as He is.

It is a faithful saying, If we be dead with Him, we shall also live with Him: if we suffer, we shall also reign with Him.

Fear not, little flock: it is your Father's good pleasure to give you the Kingdom.

Eye hath not seen, nor ear heard, neither have entered into the heart of men, the things which God hath prepared for them that love Him.

Yet a little while, and He that shall come will come, and will not tarry. Even so, come, Lord Jesus.

SENTENCES,

Which may be read during the collection for the poor.

Remember the words of the Lord Jesus, how He said, It is more blessed to give than to receive.

Ye know the grace of our Lord Jesus Christ, that, though He was rich, yet for our sakes He became poor, that ye through His poverty might be rich.

To do good and to communicate forget not: for with such sacrifices God is well pleased.

Every man according as he purposeth in his heart, so let him give; not grudgingly, or of necessity: for God loveth a cheerful giver.

If there be first a willing mind, it is accepted according to that a man hath, and not according to that he hath not.

Remember the words of the Lord Jesus, how He said, Ye have the poor with you always, and whensoever ye will ye may do them good.

As we have therefore opportunity, let us do good unto all men, especially unto them who are of the Household of Faith.

For the administration of this service not only supplieth the want of the saints, but is abundant also by many thanksgivings unto God.

God is not unrighteous to forget your work and labour of love, which ye have shewed toward His name, in that ye have ministered to the saints, and do minister.

Thanks be to God for His unspeakable gift.

THE FORM

OF

Administering the Sacrament of Baptism.

I.

Invocation.

Our help is in the Name of the Lord, who made heaven and earth. Amen.

Address.

Do you present this child to be baptized?

Answer: We do.

Our Lord hath shewed us in what poverty and misery we are all born, when He saith that we must be born again. For if it is necessary that our nature be renewed, in order that we may enter the Kingdom of God: This signifies that it is originally guilty and depraved. Thus He teacheth us that we must humble ourselves, and become displeased with ourselves; and thus He prepares us to desire and seek His grace: whereby all the depravity and guilt of our former nature shall be done away. For we are not capable of receiving that grace, unless we be first emptied of all confidence in our own strength, wisdom, and righteousness, even so as to condemn all that is in ourselves.

Now when Our Lord hath shewed us our misery, He doth likewise comfort us by His mercy: promising to regenerate us by His Holy Spirit in a new life, that shall be to us as it were an entrance into His Kingdom. This regeneration consists of these two parts: First, That we do renounce ourselves, not following our own reason, our own pleasure, and our own will; but bringing into subjection our understanding and affections to the wisdom and righteousness of God; mortifying all that is of us and of our flesh. And secondly, That we follow God's light, obeying and delighting ourselves in His good pleasure, as He manifests it by His Word, and leads us to it by His Spirit. The fulfilment of both these things rests in our Lord Jesus Christ; Whose passion and death are of such power, that participating in them, we become as it were buried unto sin, that our carnal lusts may be mortified and slain. So too by the power of His resurrection we are raised to newness of life in God, by so much as His Spirit conducts and governs us, to work in us the things that are well-pleasing to Him. But the first and principal point of our salvation is, that by His mercy He remits to us all our offences, not imputing them unto us, but destroying even the remembrance of them, that they come not into account at His judgment.

These graces are all conferred upon us, when God is pleased to incorporate us into His Church by Baptism. For in this Sacrament He doth witness to us the remission of our sins. And for this cause He hath ordained the sign of water, figuring to us that as by this element the stains of the body are cleansed, so He is willing to wash and purify our souls, that no spot appear any longer upon them. And also He doth represent to us here our regeneration; which, as hath been said, consists in the mortifying of our flesh, and the spiritual life, which He produces in us. Thus we receive in Baptism a twofold grace and benefit from our God; provided that we destroy not the virtue of this sacrament by our ingratitude: to wit, That we have here a sure testimony that God is willing to be our propitiated Father, not imputing to us our sins and offences; and secondly, that He will assist us by His Holy Spirit, that we may fight against the devil, sin, and the lusts of our flesh, even to have the victory over them, and to live in the liberty of His kingdom, which is the kingdom of righteousness and peace. Since then it is so, that these two things are accomplished in us by the grace of Jesus Christ, it follows that the virtue and the substance of Baptism are included in Him. And in fact we have no other washing than His blood: and we have no other renewal than in His death and resurrection; but as He communicates to us His riches and blessings by His Word, so too He distributes them to us by His Sacraments.

But our gracious God is not content to have adopted us for

His children, and received us into the communion of His
Church: He hath chosen more fully to extend His goodness
over us; and this by promising that He will be our God, and
the God of our seed, unto a thousand generations. And although the children of believers belong to the corrupt race of
Adam, He nevertheless doth not fail to accept them by virtue
of this Covenant, and adopt them into the number of His
People. Hence from the beginning He hath chosen that in
His Church the children should receive the sign of circumcision, whereby He then represented all that to-day is manifested
in Baptism. And as He commanded them that they should
be circumcised, so He adopted them for His children, and
called Himself their God, as He was the God of their fathers.

Now, therefore, since the Lord Jesus came down to earth,
not to diminish the grace of God His Father, but to enlarge
the covenant of salvation which then was confined to the people of the Jews, so as to include the whole world: there can
be no doubt that our children are the heirs of that life which
He hath promised, And for this cause St. Paul hath said, that
they are sanctified of God from the womb, that they may be
distinguished from the children of heathen and unbelievers.
And therefore our Lord Jesus Christ received the children who
were brought to Him, as it is written in the Gospel:

Then were there brought unto Him little children, that He
should put His hands on them, and pray: and the disciples rebuked them. But Jesus said, Suffer little children, and forbid
them not, to come unto Me; for of such is the kingdom of
heaven.

Since then He declares that the kingdom of heaven belong-
eth unto them; since He layeth His hands upon them, and
commendeth them to God His Father: He doth sufficiently
teach us, that we must not exclude them from His Church.
Therefore in pursuance of this rule, we shall receive this child
into His Church, to the end that he may be made partaker of
the blessings which God hath promised to the faithful. And
first of all we shall present *him* to God by our prayers, humbly
saying with all our hearts thus:

Prayer.

Lord God, Eternal and Almighty Father, since it hath
pleased Thee of Thine infinite mercy to promise that Thou
wilt be a God to us and to our children: We pray Thee to
confirm this grace unto the child here present, begotten and
born of parents whom Thou hast called into Thy Church. And

since *he* is offered and consecrated unto Thee by us, wilt Thou receive *him* into Thine holy protection, declaring Thyself to be *his* God and Saviour, forgiving *him* the original sin whereof the whole race of Adam is guilty; and sanctifying *him* by Thy Holy Spirit, so that when *he* shall come to years of discretion, *he* shall know and worship Thee as *his* only God, and glorify Thee throughout all *his* life. And to obtain such mercies, wilt Thou be pleased to incorporate *him* into the communion of our Lord Jesus Christ, that *he* may have a part in all His benefits, as a member of His Body. Grant, Father of mercies, that the Baptism we confer upon *him* according to Thine Ordinance, may produce its fruit and manifest its power, as Thou hast declared in the Gospel of Thy Son: Who hath taught us to say:

Our Father which art in heaven, Hallowed be Thy name. Thy kingdom come. Thy will be done in earth, as it is in heaven. Give us this day our daily bread. And forgive us our debts, as we forgive our debtors. And lead us not into temptation, but deliver us from evil: For Thine is the kingdom, and the power, and the glory, for ever. Amen.

As this child is to be received into the fellowship of the Christian Church, you do promise, when *he* is come to years of discretion, to instruct *him* in the doctrine embraced by God's People, and summarily comprehended in our common Confession of Faith, to wit:

I believe in God the Father Almighty, Maker of heaven and earth: and in Jesus Christ His only Son, our Lord; who was conceived by the Holy Ghost, born of the Virgin Mary, suffered under Pontius Pilate, was crucified, dead, and buried; He descended into hell; the third day He rose again from the dead; He ascended into heaven, and sitteth on the right hand of God the Father Almighty; from thence He shall come to judge the quick and the dead. I believe in the Holy Ghost; the Holy Catholic Church, the Communion of Saints; the forgiveness of sins; the resurrection of the body; and the life everlasting. Amen.

You promise that you will teach this child to read the Word of God. You will instruct *him* in the principles of our holy Religion, as contained in the Scriptures of the Old and New Testament. You will teach *him* to repeat the Catechism, the Apostles' Creed, and the Lord's Prayer. You will pray with and for this child; you will set an example of piety and godliness before *him*; and endeavour, by all the means of God's appointment, to bring *him* up in the nurture and admonition of the Lord.

These promises being made, the child shall be named; and the Minister calling him by his name, shall say:

I baptize thee in the Name of the Father, and of the Son, and of the Holy Ghost.

As he pronounces these words, he is to baptize the child with water, by pouring or sprinkling on the face of the child, without adding any other ceremony: and the whole shall be concluded with prayer.   CALVIN.

For the concluding prayer, or Thanksgiving, see the succeeding forms.

II.

Invocation.

Our help is in the Name of the Lord, who made heaven and earth. Amen.

Address.

Do ye here present this child to be baptized, earnestly desiring that *he* may be engrafted in the mystical body of Jesus Christ?

Answer: Yea, we require the same.

Then let us consider, dearly beloved, how Almighty God hath not only made us His children by adoption, receiving us into the fellowship of His Church: but also hath promised that He will be our God, and the God of our children, unto a thousand generations. Which promise, confirmed to His People in the Old Testament by the Sacrament of Circumcision, He hath renewed to us in His New Testament by the Sacrament of Baptism: giving us thereby to know, that our infants belong to Him by covenant, and therefore ought not to be deprived of those holy signs and badges, whereby His children are known from unbelievers.

Neither is it requisite that all those who receive this Sacrament should have the use of understanding and faith: but chiefly that they be contained under the name of God's People, so that remission of sins in the blood of Christ Jesus doth pertain unto them by the promise of God. This is most evident from the words of St. Paul, who pronounces the children begotten and born, either of the parents being faithful, to be clean and holy. Also our Saviour Christ admitteth children to His presence, embracing and blessing them. Which testimonies of the Holy Ghost assure us, that infants are of the number of God's People, and that remission of sins doth also belong to them in Christ. Therefore they can not without injury be debarred from the common sign of God's children. And yet this outward action is not of such necessity, that the lack thereof should be hurtful to their salvation; if, prevented by death, they may not be presented to the Church. But we, having respect to that obedience which Christians owe to the voice and ordinance of Christ Jesus, who commanded to preach to and baptize all, without exception, do judge them only unworthy of any fellowship with Him, who contemptuously refuse such ordinary means as His wisdom hath appointed to the instruction of our dull senses.

Further, it is evident that Baptism was ordained to be ministered in the element of water, to teach us that, like as water outwardly doth wash away the filth of the body, so inwardly doth the virtue of Christ's blood cleanse our souls from that corruption and deadly poison wherewith by nature we were infected; whose venomous dregs, although they continue in this our flesh, yet by the merits of His death are not imputed unto us, because the righteousness of Jesus Christ is made ours by Baptism. Not that we deem any such virtue or power to be included in the visible water, or outward action; for many have been baptized, and yet never inwardly cleansed: But that our Saviour Christ, who commanded Baptism to be ministered, will, by the power of His Holy Spirit, effectually work in the hearts of His Elect, in time convenient, all that is meant and signified by the same. And this the Scripture calls our regeneration; which consists chiefly in these two points: mortification, that is to say a resisting of the rebellious lusts of the flesh; and newness of life, whereby we continually strive to walk in the pureness and perfection wherewith we are clad in Baptism.

And though in the journey of this life, we are assailed with many foes, yet do we not fight without fruit. For this constant battle which we wage against sin, death, and hell, is a most infallible argument that God the Father, mindful of His promise made unto us in Christ Jesus, doth not only give us desire and courage to resist them, but also assurance to overcome. Wherefore, dearly beloved, it is not only necessary that we be once baptized, but also it profiteth much to be often present at this ministration: that being put in mind of the league and covenant made between God and us, that He will be our God, and we His People, He our Father, and we His children, we may have occasion to try as well our past lives as our present conversation; and to prove ourselves, whether we stand fast in the faith of God's Elect, or have strayed from Him through unbelief and ungodly lives. If our consciences do thus accuse us, yet by hearing the loving promises of our heavenly Father, who calls all men to mercy by repentance, we may henceforth walk more warily in our vocation. Moreover ye that be fathers and mothers, should take peculiar comfort in seeing your children thus received into the bosom of Christ's Congregation: whereby you are admonished to nourish and bring up the children of God's favour and mercy, over whom His fatherly providence continually watches.

And as this ought greatly to rejoice you, knowing that nothing can happen unto them without His good pleasure, so should it make you diligent and careful to nurture and instruct them in the true knowledge and fear of God. Wherein if ye be negligent, ye do not only injure your own children, hiding from them the good will and pleasure of Almighty God their Father: but also you heap upon yourselves judgment, in suffering His children, bought with the blood of His dear Son, so treacherously for lack of knowledge to turn away from Him. Hence it is your duty with all diligence to provide that your children, in due time, be instructed in all knowledge necessary for a true Christian: chiefly that they be taught to rest upon the righteousness of Christ Jesus alone, and to abhor and flee all superstition and idolatry. And now to the intent that we may be assured that you, the parents of this child, consent to the performance of all this: Declare here, before the face of God's Congregation, the sum of that Faith wherein ye believe, and will instruct your child.

Then the father, or in his absence the godfather, shall rehearse the articles of his faith, as follows:

I believe in God the Father Almighty, Maker of heaven and earth: and in Jesus Christ His only Son our Lord; who was conceived by the Holy Ghost, born of the Virgin Mary, suffered under Pontius Pilate, was crucified, dead, and buried; He descended into hell; the third day He rose again from the dead; He ascended into heaven, and sitteth on the right hand of God the Father Almighty; from thence He shall come to judge the quick and the dead. I believe in the Holy Ghost; the holy Catholic Church, the Communion of Saints; the forgiveness of sins; the resurrection of the body; and the life everlasting. Amen.

Then follows this

Prayer.

Almighty and Everlasting God, who of Thine infinite mercy and goodness hast promised unto us that Thou wilt be not only our God, but also the God and Father of our children: We beseech Thee that having called us to be partakers of this

Thy great mercy, in the fellowship of faith, it may please Thee to sanctify with Thy Spirit and to receive into the number of Thy children, this infant, whom we shall baptize according to Thy Word : That *he*, coming to perfect age, may confess Thee the only true God, and Jesus Christ whom thou hast sent ; and may so serve Him, and be profitable unto His Church, in the whole course of *his* life, that this life ended *he* may be brought, as a lively member of His body, unto the full fruition of Thy joys in the heavens : where Thy Son, our Saviour Christ, reigneth with Thee and the Holy Ghost, world without end. And in His name we pray, as He hath taught us, saying :

Our Father which art in heaven, Hallowed be Thy Name. Thy kingdom come. Thy will be done in earth, as it is in heaven. Give us this day our daily bread. And forgive us our debts, as we forgive our debtors. And lead us not into temptation, but deliver us from evil. For thine is the kingdom, and the power, and the glory, for ever. Amen.

When they have prayed in this sort, the Minister is to exhort the parents to the careful performance of their duty : requiring,

You promise that you will teach this child to read the word of God ; that you will instruct *him* in the principles of our holy religion, as contained in the Scriptures of the Old and New Testament ; that you will teach *him* to repeat the Catechism, the Apostles' Creed, and the Lord's Prayer ; that you will pray with and for this child ; that you will set an example of piety and godliness before *him*, and endeavour, by all the means of God's appointment, to bring *him* up in the nurture and admonition of the Lord.

These promises being made, the child shall be named, and the Minister calling him by his name, shall say,

I baptize thee, in the Name of the Father, and of the Son, and of the Holy Ghost.

As he pronounces these words, he is to baptize the child with water, by pouring or sprinkling it on the face of the child without adding any other ceremony : and the whole shall be concluded with prayer.

Thanksgiving.

We lift up our eyes unto Thee, Most Holy and Merciful Father ! Who not only dost bless us with the common benefits bestowed upon mankind, but also dost lavish the precious and wonderful gifts of Thy Gospel upon us : and we give Thee most humble thanks for Thine infinite goodness : that Thou hast numbered us among Thy Saints, and of Thy free

grace called our children unto Thee; marking them with
this Sacrament, as a singular token and badge of Thy love.
Wherefore, most loving Father! though we deserve not so
great a benefit, we beseech Thee for Christ's sake to confirm
Thy favour more and more towards us: and take into Thy
tuition and defence, this child whom we offer and present unto
Thee with our common supplications. Suffer *him* never to
fall into ingratitude, and to lose the force of Baptism; but
may *he* perceive Thee continually to be *his* Merciful Father,
through Thine Holy Spirit working in *his* heart; by whose
divine power *he* may so prevail against Satan, that in the end
obtaining the victory, *he* may be exalted into the liberty of
Thy Kingdom. Amen.   KNOX.

III.

Address.

Baptism is an holy Sacrament instituted by Christ: in which
a person professing the Christian Faith, or the infant of such,
is baptized with water into the name of the Father, and of the
Son, and of the Holy Ghost: in signification and solemnization
of the holy covenant in which as a believer, or the seed of believers, he giveth up himself, or is by the parent given up, to
God the Father, Son, and Holy Ghost: to believe in, love,
and fear this blessed Trinity, against the flesh, the devil, and
the world. Thus he is solemnly entered a visible member of
Christ and His Church, a child of God, and an heir of heaven.
How great now is this mercy, and how great the duty that is
before you! Is it a small *mercy* for this child to be accepted
into the covenant of God, and washed from *his* original sin in
the blood of Christ—which is signified and sealed by this
sacramental washing in water :—to be accepted as a member of
Christ and of His Church, where He vouchsafes His protection and provision, and the means and Spirit of grace, and the
renewed pardon of sin upon repentance? The *duty* on your
part is, first to see that you are stedfast in the faith and covenant of Christ; that you perish not yourself; that your child is
indeed the child of a believer: And then you are believingly
and thankfully to dedicate your child to God, and to enter *him*
into the covenant in which you stand. And you must know
that your faith, and consent, and dedication, will suffice for
your children no longer than until they come to age themselves: and then they must own their baptismal covenant, and
personally renew it, and consent and give themselves up to
God or else they will not be owned by Christ. You must
therefore acquaint them with the doctrine of the Gospel as they

grow up, and with the covenant now made: and bring them up in the fear of the Lord. And when they are actually penitent believers, they must present themselves to the Pastors of the Church, to be approved and received into the communion of the adult believers.

The Minister shall here say to the Parent, and the Parent answer, as followeth :

And now because these promises are made only to the faithful and to their seed, and because no man can sincerely dedicate his child to that God in whom he believeth not himself: I therefore require you to make profession of your own faith.

Do you believe in God the Father Almighty, Maker of heaven and earth: And in Jesus Christ His only Son our Lord; who was conceived by the Holy Ghost, born of the Virgin Mary, suffered under Pontius Pilate, was crucified, dead, and buried; He descended into hell; the third day He rose again from the dead; He ascended into heaven, and sitteth on the right hand of God the Father Almighty; from thence He shall come to judge the quick and the dead?

Do you believe in the Holy Ghost; the Holy Catholic Church, the Communion of Saints; the forgiveness of sins; the resurrection of the body, and the life everlasting ?

Answer: All this I unfeignedly believe.

Do you repent of your sins, and renounce the flesh, the devil, and the world, and consent to the Covenant of Grace, giving up yourself to God the Father, Son, and Holy Ghost, as your Creator and reconciled Father, your Redeemer and your Sanctifier ?

Answer : I do.

Do you here solemnly promise, that, if God continue this child with you till he be capable of instruction, you will faithfully endeavour to acquaint him with the covenant in which he was here engaged by you, and to instruct and exhort him that he perform this covenant as he looks for the blessings upon it, or to escape the curses and wrath of God ; that he renounce the flesh, the world, and the devil, and live not after them ; and that he believe in this one God in three Persons, the Father, Son, and Holy Ghost, his Creator, Redeemer, and Sanctifier ; that he resign himself to Him as his absolute owner, and obey Him as his supreme Governor, and love Him as his most gracious Father, hoping to enjoy Him as his felicity in endless glory ?

Answer : I will faithfully endeavour it.

Will you to this end faithfully endeavour to cause him to learn the articles of the Christian Faith, the Lord's Prayer, and the Ten Commandments; and to read and hear the holy Scriptures, and to attend on the public Preaching of God's Word? Will you endeavour by your own teaching, and example, and restraint, to keep him from wickedness, and train him up in a holy life?

Answer: I will faithfully endeavour it, by the help of God.

Then let the Minister pray thus:

PRAYER.

O Most Merciful Father! by the first Adam sin entered into the world, and death by sin; and we are all by nature children of wrath. But Thou hast given Thy only Son to be the seed of the woman, the Saviour of the world, the Captain of our salvation; to put away sin by the sacrifice of Himself, and to wash us in His blood, and reconcile us unto Thee, and to renew us by the Holy Ghost, and to bruise Satan under our feet. In Him Thou hast established the Covenant of Grace, and hast appointed this holy Sacrament of Baptism for our solemn entrance into the bonds of the Covenant, and instating us in the blessings of it, which Thou extendest to the faithful and their seed. We dedicate and offer this child to Thee, to be received into Thy Covenant and Thy Church. We beseech Thee to accept him as a member of thy Son, and wash him in His blood from the guilt of sin, as the flesh is washed by this water. Be reconciled to him, and take him for Thy child. Renew him in the image of Thy Son; make him a fellow-citizen with the Saints, and of Thy household. Protect him and provide for him as Thine own, and finally preserve him to Thy heavenly Kingdom: Through Jesus Christ our Lord and Saviour. Amen.

Then the Minister shall ask of the parent the name of the child to be baptized; and naming him, shall say:

I baptize thee, in the Name of the Father, and of the Son, and of the Holy Ghost.

And he shall thus declare:

This child is now received by Christ's appointment into His Church, and solemnly entered into the holy Covenant; and engaged, if he lives to the use of reason, to rise with Christ to newness of life, being buried with Him by Baptism; and to bear His Cross, and confess Christ crucified, and manfully to fight under His banner against the flesh, the devil, and the world, and to continue His faithful soldier and servant to the death, that he may receive the crown of life.

Then he shall give thanks and pray.]

Thanksgiving.

We give Thee thanks, Most Merciful Father! that when we had broken Thy law, and were condemned by it, Thou didst give us a Saviour, and eternal life in Him; and hast extended Thy Covenant of Grace to believers and to their seed; and hast now received this child into Thy covenant and Thy Church, as a member of Christ by this Sacrament of regeneration. We beseech Thee, let him grow up in holiness; and when he comes to years of discretion, let Thy Spirit reveal unto him the mysteries of the Gospel, and the riches of Thy love in Jesus Christ: and cause him to renew and perform the covenant that he hath now made, and to resign himself, and all that he hath, entirely unto Thee his Lord, to be subject and obedient to Thee his Governor, and to love Thee his Father, with all his heart, and soul, and might. May he ever adhere unto Thee, and delight in Thee, as the portion of his soul; desiring and hoping to enjoy Thee in everlasting glory. Save him from the lusts and allurements of the flesh; the temptations of the devil; the pleasure, profit, and honour of the world; from all the corruptions of his own heart, and all the hurtful violence of his foes. Keep him in communion with Thy saints, in the love and use of Thy Word and worship. May he deny himself and take up his cross, and follow Christ, the Captain of his salvation, and be faithful unto the death, and then receive the crown of life, through Jesus Christ our Saviour. Amen.   BAXTER.

IV.

Address.

The principal parts of the doctrine of Holy Baptism are these three: first, That we with our children are conceived and born in sin, and therefore are children of wrath; insomuch that we can not enter into the Kingdom of God, except we are born again: which is signified by the application of water in the Name of the Father, and of the Son, and of the Holy Ghost. Secondly, Holy Baptism witnesseth and sealeth unto us the washing away of our sins through Jesus Christ. For when we are baptized in the Name of the Father: God the Father sealeth unto us that He doth make an eternal

5

Covenant of Grace with us, and adopts us for His children and heirs. And when we are baptized in the Name of the Son : God the Son sealeth unto us that He doth wash us in His blood from all our sins; so that we are accounted righteous before God. And in like manner, when we are baptized in the Name of the Holy Ghost: God the Holy Ghost assures us that He will dwell in us, and apply that which we have in Christ, namely, the washing away of our sins, and the daily renewing of our lives, till we shall finally be presented without spot or wrinkle among the Elect in life eternal. Thirdly, Whereas in all covenants there are contained two parts, therefore are we through Baptism obliged unto new obedience : namely, that we cleave to this one God, Father, Son, and Holy Ghost; that we forsake the world, crucify our old nature, and walk in a new and holy life.

And if we sometimes through weakness fall into sin, we must not therefore despair of God's mercy, nor continue in sin, since Baptism is a seal and undoubted testimony, that we have an eternal Covenant of Grace with God.

And although our young children do not understand these things, they are not therefore to be excluded from Baptism. For as they are without their knowledge partakers of the condemnation in Adam, so are they again received unto grace in Christ. For God said unto Abraham, the father of all the faithful, and therefore unto us and our children, I will establish My Covenant between Me and thee, and thy seed after thee in their generations, for an everlasting covenant; to be a God unto thee, and to thy seed after thee. This is confirmed by the Apostle Peter, saying, For the promise is unto you, and to your children. Therefore God formerly commanded them to be circumcised, which was a seal of the covenant, and of the righteousness of faith. And therefore Christ also embraced them, laid His hands upon them, and blessed them.

Forasmuch then as Baptism is come in the place of circumcision, infants are to be baptized, as heirs of the Kingdom of God, and of His Covenant. And parents are in duty bound, further to instruct their children herein, when they shall arrive at years of discretion. That therefore this holy Ordinance of God may be administered to His glory, to our comfort, and to the edification of His Church : let us call upon His holy name.

Prayer.

O Almighty and Eternal God, we beseech Thee that Thou wilt be pleased of Thine infinite mercy graciously to look upon these children ; and incorporate them by Thy Holy Spirit into

Thy Son, Jesus Christ: that they may be buried with Him unto His death, and be raised with Him in newness of life; that they may daily follow Him, joyfully bearing their cross, and cleave unto Him in true faith, firm hope, and ardent love; that they may with a comfortable sense of Thy favour leave this life, which is nothing but a continual death; and at the last day appear without terror before the judgment-seat of Christ Thy Son: Through Jesus Christ our Lord, Who with Thee and the Holy Ghost, one only God, lives and reigns for ever. Amen.

An Exhortation,

To the Parents, and those who come with them to Baptism.

Beloved in the Lord Jesus Christ, you have heard that Baptism is an Ordinance of God, to seal unto us and to our seed His covenant. Therefore it must be used for that end, and not out of custom or superstition. That it may be then manifest that you are thus minded, you are to answer sincerely to these questions:

First, Do you acknowledge that, although our children are conceived and born in sin, and therefore under condemnation: yet they are sanctified* in Christ, and therefore, as members of His Church, ought to be baptized?

Secondly, Do you acknowledge the doctrine which is contained in the Old and New Testament, and in the articles of the Christian faith, and which is taught here in this Christian Church, to be the true and complete doctrine of salvation?

Thirdly, Do you promise and intend to see these children, when come to years of discretion, instructed and brought up in the aforesaid doctrine, or help or cause them to be instructed therein, to the utmost of your power?

Answer. Yes.

Then the Minister of God's Word, in baptizing, shall say:

N., I baptize thee, in the name of the Father, and of the Son, and of the Holy Ghost. Amen.

Thanksgiving.

Almighty God and Merciful Father, we thank and praise Thee that Thou hast promised to forgive us and our children all our sins, through the blood of Thy beloved Son Jesus

---

* *My children*, Ezek. xvi. 21. *They are holy*, 1 Cor. vii. 14.

Christ; and to receive us through The Holy Ghost as members of Thy Son, and to adopt us as thy children. We bless and praise Thee that Thou hast sealed and confirmed these promises unto us by Holy Baptism. We beseech Thee, through the same Son of Thy love, that Thou wilt be pleased always to govern these baptized children by Thy Holy Spirit; that they may be piously brought up in the nurture and admonition of the Lord; that they then may acknowledge Thy fatherly goodness and mercy, which thou hast shewn to them and us; and live in all righteousness under our only Teacher, King, and High Priest, Jesus Christ; and manfully fight against and overcome sin, the devil, and his whole dominion: to the end that they may eternally praise and magnify Thee, and Thy Son Jesus Christ, together with the Holy Ghost, the one only true God. Amen.

REFORMED DUTCH LITURGY.

THE FORM

OF

Administering the Sacrament of Baptism

TO ADULT PERSONS.

After repeating the first four paragraphs of the preceding office, the Minister proceeds thus :

However children of Christian parents, although they understand not this mystery, must be baptized, by virtue of the Covenant : yet it is not lawful to baptize those who are come to years of discretion, except they first be sensible of their sins, and make confession both of their repentance and their faith in Christ. For this cause our Lord Jesus Christ commanded His disciples to teach all nations, and then to baptize them, in the Name of the Father, and of the Son, and of the Holy Ghost; adding this promise, He that believeth and is baptized shall be saved. Accordingly, the Apostles baptized none who were of years of discretion, but such as made confession of their faith and repentance. Therefore it is not lawful now to baptize any adult persons, but those who have been taught the mysteries of Holy Baptism, and are able to give an account of their faith by the confession of the mouth.

Since then you, N., are desirous of this holy sacrament, as a seal of your engrafting into the Church of God ; that it may appear that you do not only receive the Christian Religion of which you now make confession, but do, through the grace of God, intend and purpose to lead a life according to the same; you are sincerely to give answer before God and His Church :

First. Dost thou believe in the only true God, distinct in three Persons, Father, Son, and Holy Ghost; Who hath made heaven and earth, and all that in them is, of nothing, and still maintains and governs them, insomuch that nothing comes to pass, either in heaven or on earth, without His divine will?

Answer, Yes.

Secondly. Dost thou acknowledge that thou art conceived and born in sin, and therefore art a child of wrath, by nature wholly incapable of doing any good, and prone to all evil; and that thou hast frequently, both in thought, word, and deed, transgressed the commandments of the Lord; and art thou heartily sorry for these sins?

Answer, Yes.

Thirdly. Dost thou believe that Christ, Who is the true and eternal God, and very Man, is given thee of God to be thy Saviour; and that thou dost receive by this faith remission of sins in His blood; and that thou art made by the power of the Holy Ghost a member of Jesus Christ and of His Church?

Answer, Yes.

Fourthly. Dost thou assent to all the articles of the Christian Religion, as they are here taught in this Christian Church, according to the Word of God; and purpose stedfastly to continue in the same to the end of thy life; and also dost thou reject all heresies and schisms, repugnant to this doctrine; and promise to persevere in the communion of our Christian Church, not only in the hearing of the Word, but also in the use of the Lord's Supper?

Answer, Yes.

Hast thou taken a firm resolution always to lead a Christian life; to forsake the world and its evil lusts, as is becoming the members of Christ and of His Church; and to submit thyself to all Christian admonitions?

Answer, Yes.

The good and gracious God mercifully grant His grace and blessing to this your purpose, through Jesus Christ. Amen.

Then the Minister of God's Word, in baptizing, shall say:

N., I baptize thee in the Name of the Father, and of the Son, and of the Holy Ghost. Amen.

THE FORM

The Admission of Baptized Persons

TO

THE TABLE OF THE LORD.

"Children born within the pale of the visible Church, and dedicated to God in Baptism, are under the inspection and government of the Church; and are to be taught to read and repeat the Catechism, the Apostles' Creed, and the Lord's Prayer. They are to be taught to pray, to abhor sin, to fear God, and to obey the Lord Jesus Christ. And when they come to years of discretion, if they be free from scandal, appear sober and steady, and to have sufficient knowledge to discern the Lord's Body, they ought to be informed it is their duty and their privilege to come to the Lord's Supper.

"The years of discretion in young Christians can not be precisely fixed. This must be left to the prudence of the Eldership. The officers of the Church are the judges of the qualifications of those to be admitted to sealing ordinances; and of the time when it is proper to admit young Christians to them.

"Those who are to be admitted to sealing ordinances, shall be examined as to their knowledge and piety."

DIRECTORY FOR WORSHIP, c. IX.

[The following mode of Admission, taken from Formularies of Presbyterian Churches, is used by them in connection with the Service preparatory to the celebration of the Lord's Supper]

Invocation.

Our help is in the Name of the Lord, who made heaven and earth. Amen.

Preface.

Thus saith the Lord that made thee, and formed thee from the womb, which will help thee, Fear not, O Jacob, my servant, and thou Jeshurun, whom I have chosen. For I will pour water upon him that is thirsty, and floods upon the dry ground: I will pour my Spirit upon thy seed, and my blessing upon thine offspring; and they shall spring up as among the grass, as willows by the water-courses. One shall say, I am the Lord's; and another shall subscribe himself with his hand unto the Lord, and surname himself by the name of Israel.

Address to the Congregation.

Brethren, we are here met for the admission of these young persons, who have been examined as to their knowledge and piety, to the Table of the Lord. They will publicly ratify in your hearing the engagements of their Baptism, and be received to the full participation of the benefits of the Covenant of Grace.

This occasion is one of solemn interest for each of them: and such also let it be for each of you. Let your thoughts revert to the vows that you have taken, and the privileges that you have obtained, in the communion and fellowship of Christ and of His Body the Church. To this end let us with one accord seek the blessing of the Spirit of God.

Prayer.

Almighty and most Merciful God! We give Thee hearty thanks, that Thou hast called us to the knowledge of Thyself, in Jesus Christ our Lord; and hast vouchsafed to make us partakers of the great and precious promises of Thy holy Word. We praise Thee for the certain assurance, that these promises are unto us, and to our children, and to all that are afar off, even as many as Thy grace shall call. O Merciful God, we have believed the witness of Thy Word. We have dedicated these children from their infancy to Thee. We have sought for them admission to Thy Church by Holy Baptism. We have taught them Thy saving Truth; and now that they have reached years of discretion, we come with them, to witness their willing renewal of the sacred vows that bind them to Thy Covenant. Lord, we beseech Thee, help them at this solemn hour. Work in them both to will and to do of Thy good pleasure. Make them sincere in repentance, strong in faith, stedfast in hope, and fervent in charity. Receive them into the communion of Thy Son Jesus Christ our Lord; and enable them to persevere unto the end, by the grace of Thy Holy Spirit. Amen.

Then the Minister addressing the Candidates says:·

You that desire to be admitted to the Table of the Lord, are you so fully persuaded of the truths of the Gospel in which you have been taught, that you are ready to suffer all things, sooner than renounce the profession you now make?

Answer: Yes.

Have you examined your own hearts, and are you determined to forsake sin, and to order your lives in obedience to God's law?

Answer: Yes.

Do you promise that, for the strengthening of your faith and piety, you will give yourselves to the careful study and meditation of the Word of God, and to prayer; to a regular attendance upon the assemblies of His People; and to all other means that Providence shall furnish, for the advancement of your salvation?

Answer: Yes.

Do you then sincerely and with your whole hearts confirm and ratify the vows of your Baptism, that bind you to renounce the world with all its vanities, to resist your evil passions, to consecrate yourselves to God, your Father, Saviour, and Sanctifier; and to live in temperance, righteousness, and holiness all your days?

Answer: Yes.

Then the Minister says:

In view of these your promises, I admit you to the Table of the Supper of our Lord Jesus Christ, that you may enjoy all the privileges of the Covenant of Grace.

May you be deeply sensible of the importance and the solemnity of the engagement that you have now entered upon, and retain the impression of it throughout your lives. Remember that it is to God, your Maker, your Redeemer, and your Judge, that these promises have been made; and that upon the care you take to fulfil them, will depend your eternal blessedness. Walk worthily, then, of your high vocation. Let the light of your good works shine before men. Labour to perfect holiness, in the fear of the Lord. Seek daily the strength of God. Nourish your souls with His Word. Be watchful unto prayer. Flee youthful snares, that would lead you away from Him.

Thus devoting yourselves to God from youth, you will be so accustomed to His service, that His yoke will seem to you easy, and His burthen light, and your joy will be found in doing His blessed will. God on His part will bless you; He will give you His peace, that passeth all understanding. The eye of the Lord will be upon you, and His ear will be open to your prayers; the blood of Jesus Christ will cleanse you from all sin. Be fearful of nothing; because greater is He that is in you, than he that is in the world. His strength will be made perfect in your weakness; you will be able to do all things through Christ who strengtheneth you. In the hour of death, you will be sustained by the hope of a joyful resurrection, and having here below your fruit unto holiness, you shall have the end everlasting life.

Then the Minister addressing the whole congregation says:

And you, Brethren, who now witness the entrance of these baptized persons upon a connection yet more close and intimate with yourselves, let your affection for them, and your earnest solicitude for their welfare, be henceforth redoubled. And let us all with one accord, as members of one Body, unite in fervent prayer, that God may pour down His grace upon us, and guide by His Holy Spirit into His perfect way.

Prayer.

The Candidates kneeling.

O Lord our God, who hast chosen to Thyself a Church on earth, and who hast promised to preserve it unto the end of the world, and finally raise it unto Thy glory: Look down in Thy goodness upon these baptized persons now prostrate before Thee, who have been solemnly admitted to the full communion and fellowship of Thy Church. Thou hadst already called them, by the promises of Thy Covenant, which are made unto us and unto our children; and granted them the seal of this privilege of Christian birth, in the ordinance of Baptism. But since the weakness of their infancy prevented the personal and voluntary dedication of themselves, they come now to confirm the vows of obedience that were taken for them, to consecrate themselves entirely to Thy service, and to beseech Thee that Thou wilt graciously regard them as Thy children. They have been taught, O God, to know Thee, their Father, Saviour, and Sanctifier. They are persuaded that there is salvation in none other, and they desire to have part in the benefits of the sacrifice of Christ, and His efficacious intercession. Accept, O Lord, these purposes of their hearts, and receive them into the communion of Thy Son. May they love Thy truth, and ever seek to know it more thoroughly, and to profess it more consistently, unto the end of their lives. May they withstand all evil, renounce the world, its vanities and delusions, and live as the heirs and citizens of heaven. May the Sacrament of which they shall partake be accompanied with a fresh outpouring of Thy grace upon them. Take possession of their hearts by Thy Holy Spirit; and at last receive them with us into Thy heavenly habitations, through our Great Redeemer and Advocate, Jesus Christ Thy Son. Amen.

Our Father, etc.

Benediction.

The blessing of God Almighty, the Father, the Son, and the Holy Ghost, be amongst you and remain with you always. Amen.   WALDENSIAN LITURGY.

THE OFFICE

FOR

The Confirmation of Marriage.

Our help is in the Name of the Lord, who made heaven and earth. Amen.

Dearly beloved Brethren, we are here gathered together in the sight of God, and in the face of His Congregation, to join together these persons in the honourable estate of Matrimony : which was instituted and authorized by God Himself in Paradise, Man being then in the state of innocency. For what time God made heaven and earth, and all that in them is, and had created and fashioned Man also in His own similitude and likeness, He said, It is not good that the Man should be alone ; I will make him an help meet for him. And the Lord God caused a deep sleep to fall upon Adam, and He took one of his ribs, and framed Eve thereof : giving us thereby to understand, that they two are one body, one flesh, and one blood. For the which cause a man leaveth father and mother, and cleaveth to his wife ; whom he ought to love, as our Saviour loveth the Church, for the which He gave His life. Likewise also it is the wife's duty, to study to please and obey her husband, serving him in all things that be godly and honest : for she is under the governance of her husband, so long as they continue both alive.

Here the Minister speaketh to the parties that shall be married, in this wise:

I require and charge you, as ye will answer at the day of judgment, when the secrets of all hearts shall be disclosed, that if either of you do know any impediment, why ye may not lawfully be joined together in matrimony, ye confess it. For be ye well assured, that so many as be joined otherwise than God's Word doth allow, are not joined together by God, neither is their matrimony lawful.

If no impediment be by them declared, then the Minister saith to the whole Congregation:

I take you to witness that be here present, beseeching you all to have good remembrance thereof: and moreover, if there be any of you which knoweth that either of these parties be contracted to any other, or knoweth any other lawful impediment, let them now make declaration thereof.

If no cause be alleged, the Minister proceedeth, saying:

Forasmuch as no man speaketh against this thing, Our Lord confirm your good purpose which He hath given you: and your beginning be in the Name of the Lord, which made heaven and earth.

You, M., do here acknowledge before God, and His holy Congregation, that you have taken and do take N., here present, for your lawful wife: you do promise to keep her, to love her and maintain her, faithfully, as a true and faithful husband is bound to do; and forsaking all other, to live holily with her, keeping faith and truth in all things, according as the Word of God and His holy Gospel doth appoint?

Answer: Even so I take her, before God, and in the presence of this Congregation.

Then the Minister to the Spouse also saith:

You, N., do here acknowledge before God and His holy Congregation, that you have taken and do take M., here present, for your lawful husband: you do promise to obey him, to love him, faithfully, as a true and faithful wife is bound to do; and forsaking all other, to live holily with him, keeping faith and truth in all things, according as the Word of God and His holy Gospel doth appoint?

Answer: Even so I take him, before God, and in the presence of this Congregation.

Then the Minister shall say:

The Father of all Mercies, who of His grace hath called you to this holy state of Marriage, bind you in true love and faithfulness all your lives.

Whom God hath joined together, let no man put asunder.

Let us all with one heart call upon God.

O God, Most Mighty, Gracious and Wise! since it hath
pleased Thee to call these persons to the holy state of Marriage: Grant them, we beseech Thee, the grace of Thy Holy
Spirit: that with true and firm faith they may live holily
together, according to Thy will, to the edification of all men,
by their pure and honest life. Bless them, as Thou blessedst
Thy faithful servants Abraham, Isaac, and Jacob: that they
may be partakers of that covenant which Thou madest with
them. Hear us, O Father of all Mercies! through Jesus Christ
our Lord. In whose Name we also pray, saying,
Our Father which art in heaven, Hallowed be Thy Name.
Thy kingdom come. Thy will be done in earth, as it is in
heaven. Give us this day our daily bread. And forgive us
our debts, as we forgive our debtors. And lead us not into
temptation, but deliver us from evil: For Thine is the kingdom, and the power, and the glory, for ever. Amen.

The Lord bless you, and keep you: The Lord make His
face shine upon you, and be gracious unto you: The Lord
lift up His countenance upon you, and give you peace. Amen.
                                                 KNOX.

II.

God be merciful unto us, and bless us, and cause His face
to shine upon us, through Jesus Christ our Lord. Amen.

In the Name of Almighty God, I demand of each of you
here present, that if you know any good reason why these persons ———— and ————, should not be joined in Marriage, ye
do now declare the same, as ye would answer before the
Searcher of hearts.

God created Man in His own image, and said, It is not
good that man should be alone — I will make a help meet
for him. He brought unto the man the woman whom He
had made. And Adam said, This is now bone of my bones,
and flesh of my flesh. Therefore shall a man leave father and
mother, and cleave unto his wife: and they twain shall be
one flesh.
Marriage, thus ordained of God in Eden, was confirmed at
the wedding in Cana of Galilee, by the gracious presence and
miraculous blessing of our divine Lord Jesus Christ: who hath
also said, What God hath joined together let not man put

asunder. Moreover, His holy Apostle Paul has commended unto the husband the example of Christ in loving His Church, and unto the wife the willing subjection of the Church unto Christ as her head. Whence we learn that Marriage is well-pleasing to God our Saviour, and most honourable to all who maintain therein a mutual love and unshaken fidelity.

I therefore, a minister of the blessed Gospel, charge and entreat you both, to seek the help of God in all your duties; that His grace may make your union fruitful of comfort in this life, and a furtherance of your everlasting salvation, to the glory of His holy Name.

Let us pray.

O Most Holy and Most Merciful Lord God, we beseech Thee for these Thy servant and handmaid; that they may, with a reverent trust in Thee, enter into the covenant of marriage, as they now propose, and truly keep all the vows which they are about to make according to Thy Word. Grant this, O our Father, with the forgiveness of our sins, through Christ Thy Son. Amen.

Then the Minister shall bid the man and the woman to join their right hands: which, being done, he shall say to the man:

Dost thou ———, take this woman ———, before God and these witnesses, to be thy wife?

The man shall answer, Yes.

Dost thou promise to love her, honour her, defend her, sustain and cherish her, in joy and in sorrow, in health and in sickness, in prosperity and in adversity? Wilt thou be faithful to her in all things as becometh a good husband, and never forsake her so long as ye both do live?

Answer: Yes.

The Minister shall then say to the woman:

Dost thou ———, take this man ———, before God and these witnesses, to be thy husband?

Answer: Yes.

Dost thou promise to love him, honour him, cherish and obey him, in joy and in sorrow, in health and in sickness, in prosperity and adversity? Wilt thou be faithful to him in all things as becometh a good wife, and never forsake him so long as ye both do live?

Answer: Yes.

[*When a ring is used.*]

To the man :

What pledge dost thou give that thou wilt perform these thy vows?

The man shows the ring.

To the woman :

Dost thou receive this ring in token of the same on thy part?

Then the man (the Minister guiding his hand) shall place the ring on the fourth finger of her left hand.

Then the Minister shall say :

Let us pray.

O God, our heavenly Father, Thou hast heard these promises of Thy servant and handmaid to each other : Mercifully condescend to unite their hearts and lives by all the grace and true affection of a happy marriage. May their love never know change, or doubt, or decay. Replenish them with Thy Holy Spirit, that they may piously live together according to Thy divine will. May they be blessed in each other, and both in the knowledge of Christ Thy Son, and may they at last enter Thy blessed Kingdom: Though Jesus Christ our Redeemer. Amen.

Then the Minister, taking their clasped hands between his, shall say :

Now in the Name of God, Father, Son, and Holy Ghost, whose servant I am, I pronounce you husband and wife.

The Lord bless you, and keep you.

The Lord make His face shine upon you, and be gracious unto you.

The Lord lift up His countenance upon you, and give you ' peace.

Then, still holding their hands, the Minister shall say to the company of witnesses :

What God hath joined together, let not man put asunder.

THE BURIAL OF THE DEAD.

THE SERVICE AT THE HOUSE.

Prefaces,

One or more of which may be read at discretion.

It is better to go to the house of mourning than to go to the house of feasting; for that is the end of all men, and the living will lay it to heart.

Let us weep with those that weep; and let our prayer also be in their calamities.

Affliction cometh not forth of the dust, neither doth trouble spring out of the ground. See now, saith the Lord, I, even I am He, and there is no God beside Me. I kill, and I make alive; I wound, and I heal; neither is there any that can deliver out of My hand.

The Lord destroyeth the hope of man. The Lord prevaileth against him, and he passeth. He changeth his countenance, and sendeth him away.

It is of the Lord's mercies that we are not consumed; because His compassions fail not. Like as a father pitieth his children, so the Lord pitieth them that fear Him. For He knoweth our frame; He remembereth that we are dust.

Though He cause grief, yet will He have compassion according to the multitude of His mercies. For He doth not afflict willingly the children of men.

Despise not the chastening of the Lord, neither faint when

6

thou art rebuked of Him: for whom the Lord loveth He chasteneth, and scourgeth every son whom He receiveth. Now no chastening for the present seemeth to be joyous but grievous; nevertheless afterward it yieldeth the peaceable fruits of righteousness unto them which are exercised thereby. Wherefore lift up the hands that hang down, and the feeble knees.

For we have not an High Priest which can not be touched with the feeling of our infirmities; but was in all points tempted like as we are, yet without sin. Let us therefore come boldly unto the throne of grace, that we may obtain mercy, and find grace to help in time of need.

Leave thy fatherless children, saith the Lord; I will preserve them alive; and let thy widows trust in Me.

A Father of the fatherless, and a Judge of the widow, is God in His holy habitation.

When my father and my mother forsake me, then the Lord will take me up.

(*For an Infant:*) And David said, While the child was yet alive, I fasted and wept, for I said, who can tell whether God will be gracious unto me, that the child may live? But now he is dead, wherefore should I fast? Can I bring him back again? I shall go to him; but he shall not return to me.

The Lord gave, and the Lord hath taken away, blessed be the Name of the Lord.

A bruised reed shall He not break, and the smoking flax shall He not quench.

Prayer.

O God, Merciful God, Father of our Lord Jesus Christ, Who hast said, Blessed are they that mourn, for they shall be comforted: Under the shadow of Thy judgments we come to Thee, and acknowledge Thee to be the Lord alone. Thou hast entered this house with Thy chastenings: Oh! be Thou nigh in Thy tender compassion to these afflicted ones. Bless Thy sorrowing servants with Thy consolations, which are neither few nor small. Convert them wholly to Thyself, and fill their bleeding hearts with Thy love. Make the night of their grief to be light by Thy grace. Deliver us Thy servants, we pray Thee, from the bondage of our sins, that we may be free from fear of death, and be ready at Thy coming. Yea, Lord! for Christ's sake, sanctify us by Thy Holy Spirit, that whether we live, we may live unto the Lord, or whether we die, we may die unto the Lord; whether we live or die, may we be the Lord's. Amen.

The grace of the Lord Jesus Christ, and the love of God, and the communion of the Holy Ghost, be with you all. Amen.

———————

THE SERVICE AT THE CHURCH.

[*If the service be performed in whole at the house, then a part of the following may be used in connection with the preceding form.*]

Upon entering the church, when all shall have taken the attitude of prayer, let the XCth Psalm be read as an

Invocation.

Lord, Thou hast been our dwelling-place in all generations. Before the mountains were brought forth, or ever Thou hadst formed the earth and the world, even from everlasting to everlasting, Thou art God. Thou turnest man to destruction; and sayest, Return, ye children of men. For a thousand years in Thy sight are but as yesterday when it is past, and as a watch in the night. Thou carriest them away as with a flood; they are as a sleep: in the morning they are like grass which groweth up. In the morning it flourisheth and groweth up; in the evening it is cut down, and withereth. For we are consumed by Thine anger, and by Thy wrath are we troubled. Thou hast set our iniquities before Thee, our secret sins in the light of Thy countenance. For all our days are passed away in Thy wrath: we spend our years as a tale that is told. The days of our years are three score years and ten; and if by reason of strength they be four score years, yet is their strength labour and sorrow; for it is soon cut off, and we fly away. Who knoweth the power of Thine anger? even according to Thy fear, so is Thy wrath. So teach us to number our days, that we may apply our hearts unto wisdom. Return, O Lord! how long? and let it repent Thee concerning Thy servants. Oh satisfy us early with Thy mercy; that we may rejoice and be glad all our days. Make us glad according to the days wherein Thou hast afflicted us, and the years wherein we have seen evil. Let Thy work appear unto Thy servants, and Thy glory unto their children. And let the beauty of the Lord our God be upon us: and establish Thou the work of our hands upon us: yea, the work of our hands establish Thou it.

Here may be sung a Funeral Hymn.

*Then let there be read two portions of Scripture, from the Gospel and the Epistles.
The following are suitable passages.*

Hear the comfortable words of the Gospel of our Saviour Jesus Christ, as they are written in the eleventh chapter of Saint John.

Then said Mârtha unto Jesus, Lord, if Thou hadst been here, my brother had not died. But I know, that even now, whatsoever Thou wilt ask of God, God will give it Thee. Jesus saith unto her, Thy brother shall rise again. Martha saith unto Him, I know that he shall rise again in the Resurrection at the last day. Jesus said unto her, I am the Resurrection, and the Life: he that believeth in Me, though he were dead, yet shall he live: and whosoever liveth and believeth in Me shall never die. Believest thou this? She saith unto Him, Yea, Lord: I believe that Thou art the Christ, the Son of God, which should come into the world.

Or this:

Hear the Gospel of our Saviour Jesus Christ, in the fifth chapter of Saint John:

Verily, verily, I say unto you, He that heareth My word, and believeth on Him that sent Me, hath everlasting life, and shall· not come into condemnation; but is passed from death unto life. Verily, verily, I say unto you, The hour is coming, and now is, when the dead shall hear the voice of the Son of God: and they that hear shall live. For as the Father hath life in himself, so hath He given to the Son to have life in Himself; and hath given Him authority to execute judgment also, because He is the Son of Man. Marvel not at this: for the hour is coming, in the which all that are in the graves shall hear His voice, and shall come forth; they that have done good, unto the Resurrection of life; and they that have done evil, unto the Resurrection of damnation.

[For an Infant.]

Hear the comfortable words of our Saviour Jesus Christ.

They brought young children to Him that He should touch them; and His disciples rebuked those that brought them. But when Jesus saw it, He was much displeased, and said unto them, Suffer the little children to come unto Me, and forbid them not, for of such is the Kingdom of Heaven. Verily I say unto you, whosoever shall not receive the Kingdom of Heaven as a little child, he shall not enter therein.

Or this:

Take heed that ye despise not one of these little ones; for I

say unto you, That in heaven their angels do always behold
the face of My Father which is in heaven. For the Son of
Man is come to save that which was lost. How think ye? if a
man have a hundred sheep, and one of them be gone astray,
doth he not leave the ninety and nine, and goeth into the
mountains, and seeketh that which is gone astray? And if so
be that he find it, verily I say unto you, he rejoiceth more of
that sheep, than of the ninety and nine which went not astray.
Even so it is not the will of your Father which is in heaven,
that one of these little ones should perish.

Then, before the second portion of Scripture, may be read one or more of these sentences:

By one man sin entered into the world, and death by sin,
and so death hath passed upon all men, because that all have
sinned.

The living know that they must die; for there is one event
unto all.

They that trust in their wealth, and boast themselves in the
multitude of their riches, none of them can by any means redeem his brother, nor give to God a ransom for him, that he
should live for ever, and not see corruption.

As a cloud is consumed and vanisheth away, so he that
goeth down to the grave shall return no more. He shall return no more to his house, neither shall his place know him
any more. His days are ended, his purposes are broken off,
even the thoughts of his heart.

Then let the second portion of Scripture be read, from 1 Corinthians XV.:

Hear also what the Apostle Paul saith:

Now is Christ risen from the dead, and become the first fruits
of them that slept. For since by man came death, by Man
came also the Resurrection of the dead. For as in Adam all
die, even so in Christ shall all be made alive. But every man
in his own order: Christ the first-fruits; afterward they that
are Christ's at His coming.—But some man will say, How are
the dead raised up? and with what body do they come? Thou
fool, that which thou sowest is not quickened, except it die:
and that which thou sowest, thou sowest not that body that
shall be, but bare grain, it may chance of wheat, or of some
other grain: but God giveth it a body as it hath pleased Him,
and to every seed his own body.—So also is the Resurrection
of the dead. It is sown in corruption, it is raised in incorruption: it is sown in dishonour, it is raised in glory: it is sown
in weakness, it is raised in power: it is sown a natural body,

it is raised a spiritual body. There is a natural body, and there is a spiritual body. And so it is written, The first man Adam was made a living soul; the last Adam was made a quickening spirit. Howbeit that was not first which is spiritual, but that which is natural; and afterward that which is spiritual. The first man is of the earth, earthy: the second Man is the Lord from heaven. As is the earthy, such are they also that are earthy; and as is the heavenly, such are they also that are heavenly. And as we have borne the image of the earthy, we shall also bear the image of the heavenly. Now this I say, brethren, that flesh and blood can not inherit the Kingdom of God; neither doth corruption inherit incorruption. Behold, I shew you a mystery: We shall not all sleep, but we shall all be changed, in a moment, in the twinkling of an eye, at the last trump: for the trumpet shall sound, and the dead shall be raised incorruptible, and we shall be changed. For this corruptible must put on incorruption, and this mortal must put on immortality. So when this corruptible shall have put on incorruption, and this mortal shall have put on immortality, then shall be brought to pass the saying that is written, Death is swallowed up in victory. O death, where is thy sting? O grave, where is thy victory? The sting of death is sin, and the strength of sin is the law. But thanks be to God which giveth us the victory, through our Lord Jesus Christ.

Or this, from Revelation XX. ·

Hear also the Revelation of St. John:

And I saw a great white throne, and Him that sat on it, from whose face the earth and the heaven fled away; and there was found no place for them. And I saw the dead, small and great, stand before God; and the books were opened: and another book was opened, which is the Book of life: and the dead were judged out of those things which were written in the books, according to their works. And the sea gave up the dead which were in it; and death and hell delivered up the dead which were in them: and they were judged every man according to their works.

Or this, from Revelation XXI.:

And I saw a new heaven and a new earth: for the first heaven and the first earth were passed away; and there was no more sea. And I John saw the Holy City, New Jerusalem, coming down from God out of heaven, prepared as a bride adorned for her husband. And I heard a great voice out of heaven, saying, Behold, the Tabernacle of God is with men, and He will dwell with them, and they shall be His People, and God Himself shall be with them, and be their God. And God shall wipe away all tears from their eyes; and there shall be no more death, neither sorrow, nor crying, neither shall there be any more pain: for the former things are passed away.

Prayer.

O God, whose days are without end, and whose mercies can not be numbered: Make us, we beseech Thee, deeply sensible of the shortness and uncertainty of human life; and let Thy Holy Spirit lead us through this vale of misery, in holiness and righteousness, all the days of our lives: that when we shall have served Thee in our generation, we may be gathered unto our fathers, having the testimony of a good conscience; in the communion of the Christian Church; in the confidence of a certain faith; in the comfort of a reasonable, religious, and holy hope; in favour with Thee our God, and in perfect charity with the world: all which we ask through Jesus Christ our Lord. Amen.

The grace of our Lord Jesus Christ be with you all. Amen.

THE SERVICE AT THE GRAVE.

Man goeth to his long home, and the mourners go about the streets.

What man is he that liveth, and shall not see death? Shall he deliver his soul from the hand of the grave?

I heard a voice from heaven saying unto me, write: Blessed are the dead which die in the Lord from henceforth. Yea, saith the Spirit, for they rest from their labours, and their works do follow them.

Blessed be the God and Father of our Lord Jesus Christ, which according to His abundant mercy hath begotten us again unto a lively hope by the Resurrection of Jesus Christ from the dead, to an inheritance incorruptible, undefiled, and that fadeth not away, reserved in heaven for you, who are kept by the power of God through faith unto salvation.

At the time of burial, the Minister shall say:

The dust returns to dust, and the spirit unto God who gave it: therefore do we now commit the body of our departed *brother* to the earth [*or* deep] until that hour when earth and sea shall give up their dead, at the coming of our Lord Jesus Christ to judge the world.

Let us pray.

Almighty and Everlasting God! we Thine unworthy servants beseech Thee for Christ's sake to have pity upon us. From the borders of the grave we cry unto Thee; for Christ's sake have mercy upon us. It hath pleased Thee to call out of this world the soul of our departed friend, whose body we have now brought for *his* burial. We humbly entreat Thee that we may with true penitence of heart receive the warning of Thy providence, and consider that for reason of our guilt it is appointed unto us to die, and that in a moment when we think not we may appear before Thee. Yea, Lord, by reason of our sins we lie in the midst of death. Spare us, O Lord, O most pitiful and long-suffering Lord God, spare us a little longer, that we may take refuge in Christ, abiding in Him, that when He shall appear we may have confidence, and not be ashamed at His coming. O Merciful God and Father of our Lord Jesus Christ, suffer none of us to live without godliness and die without hope; but constrain us mightily by Thy love: that we, being renewed by Thy grace, and accepted through Christ's intercession, may walk before Thee in newness of life, and praise Thee for ever among the Assembly of the Elect, where there shall be no more death, and sorrow and sighing shall flee away: which we implore for the sake of Him who has taught us to say,

Our Father which art in heaven, Hallowed be thy Name. Thy kingdom come. Thy will be done in earth, as it is heaven. Give us this day our daily bread. And forgive us our debts, as we forgive our debtors. And lead us not into temptation, but deliver us from evil: For Thine is the kingdom, and the power, and the glory, for ever. Amen.

Benediction.

Now the God of Peace, that brought again from the dead our Lord Jesus, that great Shepherd of the sheep, through the blood of the everlasting covenant, make you perfect in every good work to do His will, working in you that which is well-pleasing in His sight, through Jesus Christ. Amen.

THE

ORDER OF SERVICE

FOR A

Day of Humiliation, Fasting, and Prayer.

Invocation.

Our help is in the Name of the Lord, who made heaven and earth. Amen.

Preface.

Wherewith shall I come before the Lord, and bow myself before the high God? Shall I come before Him with burnt-offerings, with calves of a year old? Will the Lord be pleased with thousands of rams, or with ten thousands of rivers of oil? Shall I give my first-born for my transgression, the fruit of my body for the sin of my soul? He hath shewed thee, O man, what is good; and what doth the Lord require of thee, but to do justly, and to love mercy, and to walk humbly with thy God?

The Opening Prayer.

O Lord, Thy mercy is without measure, and the truth of Thy promise abideth for ever. Unworthy are we that Thou shouldst look upon us; but Thou hast promised to shew Thy compassion toward the most grievous offenders, whensoever they repent; and by the mouth of Thy dear Son our Lord

Jesus Christ, to give Thy Holy Spirit unto such as humbly call upon Thee. In boldness of this promise, we most humbly beseech Thee, O Father of Mercies, that it may please Thee to work in our stubborn hearts an unfeigned sorrow for our offences, a feeling of Thy grace and mercy, and an earnest desire for that righteousness in which we are bound continually to walk. But because neither we nor our prayers can stand before Thee, we fly to the obedience and perfect righteousness of Jesus Christ our only Mediator: in whom, and by whom, we ask of Thee not only the remission of our sins, and the help of Thy Spirit, but all things also that Thy wisdom knoweth to be expedient for us, and for Thy Church Universal. Amen.   KNOX.

Here may be sung a penitential Psalm.

Then follows the Reading of Scripture, out of the Old and New Testaments

The following are appropriate selections.

Isaiah i. 10–27.	St Matthew iii. 1–12.
Isaiah lviii	Hebrews iii.
Jeremiah vii. 1–20.	St. Matthew xxi 28–46.
Psalm li.	St Luke xiii. 23–35
Ezekiel xviii. 20–32.	St Luke xviii 1–14.
Daniel ix. 1–19.	St. Luke xv. 11–32.

FRENCH LITURGY.

Next the

General Prayer,

Beginning with the Prayer of our Lord.

Our Father which art in Heaven, Hallowed be Thy Name. Thy kingdom come. Thy will be done in earth, as it is in heaven. Give us this day our daily bread. And forgive us our debts, as we forgive our debtors. And lead us not into temptation, but deliver us from evil: For Thine is the kingdom, and the power, and the glory, for ever. Amen.

O Almighty, Most Just and Merciful God! we acknowledge ourselves unworthy to lift up our eyes unto heaven, as we present ourselves before Thee. For our consciences accuse us, and our sins reprove us; and we know that Thou who art a righteous Judge, must needs punish them that transgress Thy law. O Lord! when we look back and examine our whole life, we find nothing in ourselves that deserveth any other reward than eternal condemnation. But since Thou, of Thine unspeakable mercy, hast commanded us in all our necessities to call upon Thee; and hast also promised that Thou wilt hear our prayers, not for any merit of our own, for we have none, but for the merits of Thy Son, whom Thou hast ordained to be our only Mediator and Intercessor: Therefore we lay aside all confidence in man, and flee to the throne of Thy mercy, by the intercession of Thy only Son our Saviour, Jesus Christ.

O Lord! we do lament and bewail, from the bottom of our hearts, our past unthankfulness towards Thee. We remember that besides those benefits of Thine which we enjoy in common with all men as Thy creatures, Thou hast bestowed upon us many special blessings, of which we are not able in heart to conceive the value, much less in words worthily to express it. Thou hast called us to the knowledge of Thy Gospel. Thou hast released us from the hard servitude of Satan. Thou hast delivered us from all idolatry, wherein we were sunken; and hast brought us into the clear and comfortable light of Thy blessed Word. But we, most unmindful, in our prosperity, of these Thy great benefits, have neglected Thy commandments, have abused the knowledge of Thy Gospel, have followed our carnal liberty, have served our own lusts, and through our sinful lives have failed suitably to serve and honour Thee.

And now, O Lord! we do most humbly confess that we have sinned, and have most grievously displeased Thee. And if Thou, Lord! provoked with our disobedience, shouldst now deal with us as we have deserved, there remaineth nothing to be looked for, but continual plagues in this world, and hereafter eternal death and condemnation, both of body and of soul. For if we should excuse ourselves, our own consciences would accuse us before Thee, and our own disobedience and wickedness would bear witness against us. Yet, although Thou shouldst punish us more grievously still; though Thou shouldst pour upon us all those testimonies of Thy just wrath, which in time past Thou pouredst on Thy chosen people, Israel: yet could we not deny that we had justly deserved it.

But, O merciful Lord! Thou art our God, and we are Thine inheritance; Thou art our Creator, and we the work of Thy hands; Thou art our Shepherd, we Thy flock; Thou art our Redeemer, and we the people whom Thou hast redeemed; Thou art our Father, we are Thy children. Lord! be not wroth against us; punish us not in Thy sore displeasure.

Remember, O Lord! that Thy Name hath been named upon us; that we bear Thy seal and the tokens of Thy service. Perfect the work Thou hast begun in us; that all the world may know Thou art our God and merciful Deliverer. Thou knowest that the dead who are in their graves can not praise Thee; but the sorrowful spirit, the contrite heart, the conscience broken with a sense of sin, and panting for Thy grace, shall give Thee praise and glory. Thy people Israel ofttimes offended Thee, and Thou didst justly afflict them; but as oft as they returned to Thee, Thou didst receive them in mercy; and though their sins were never so great, yet didst Thou turn away Thy wrath, and the punishment prepared for them: and that for Thy Covenant's sake, which Thou madest with Thy servants Abraham, Isaac, and Jacob. Thou hast made a better Covenant with us, O heavenly Father! a Covenant on which we may lean as we appear before Thee: through the mediation of Thy dear Son Jesus Christ our Saviour, with whose most precious blood it pleased Thee that this covenant should be written, sealed, and confirmed.

Wherefore, O heavenly Father! we now, casting away all confidence in ourselves or any other creature, do flee to this most holy covenant and testament; wherein our Lord and Saviour Jesus Christ, once offering himself a sacrifice for us on the Cross, hath reconciled us to Thee for ever. Look, therefore, O merciful God! not upon the sins that we continually commit, but upon our Mediator and Peacemaker, Jesus Christ: that by His intercession Thy wrath may be pacified, and we again by Thy fatherly countenance relieved and comforted. Receive us also into Thy heavenly defence, and govern us by Thy Holy Spirit. Frame in us newness of life, wherein to laud and magnify Thy blessed Name for ever, and to live every one of us according to the several states of life whereunto Thou hast ordained us.

And, O heavenly Father! although by reason of our past sins, we are unworthy to crave any thing of Thee: yet because Thou hast commanded us to pray for all men, we most humbly beseech Thee, save and defend Thy holy Church. Be merciful to all commonwealths, countries, princes, and magistrates; and especially to this our land, and to its rulers and governors. Increase the number of godly ministers. Endue them with Thy grace, to be found faithful and prudent in their office. Bless the President of the United States, and all that be in authority. We commend also to Thy fatherly mercy all that be in poverty, exile, imprisonment, sickness, or any other kind of adversity; and chiefly those whom Thy hand hath touched with any dangerous sickness: which we beseech Thee, O Lord! of Thy mercy, when Thy blessed will is, to remove. And in the meantime grant us the grace of true repentance, stedfast faith, and constant patience: that whether we live or die, we may always continue Thine, and ever bless Thy holy Name, and be brought to the fruition of Thy Godhead. Grant these, and all our humble petitions, O merciful Father! for the sake of Thy dear Son Jesus Christ our Lord. Amen.

CALVIN.

After this Prayer a Hymn shall be sung before the

SERMON:

At the close of which another Hymn.

Then the

Closing Prayer.

Most Mighty God! Thou who from the beginning hast de-clared Thyself a consuming fire against the contemners of Thy holy precepts; yet to penitent sinners hast always shewed Thyself a favourable Father, and a God full of mercy: We Thy creatures once more confess ourselves most unworthy to open our eyes unto the heavens, far less to appear in Thy presence. For our manifold iniquities have borne witness against us, that we have declined from Thee. We have given Thy glory to creatures; we have sought support where it was not to be found: and have slighted Thy most wholesome admonitions. We are not ignorant, O Lord, that Thou art a righteous Judge, who canst not suffer iniquity long to be unpunished upon obstinate transgress-ors; especially when that after so long blindness and de-fection from Thee, so lovingly Thou callest us back, and that yet we do rebel. We have nothing, O Lord, that we may lay between us and Thy judgment, but only Thy mercy, freely offered unto us in Thy dear Son our Lord Jesus Christ. For if Thou wilt enter into judgment with Thy servants, and keep in mind our grievous offences, then can there no flesh escape condemnation. And therefore we most humbly beseech Thee, O Father of Mercies, for Christ Jesus Thy Son's sake, to take from us these stony hearts that so long have heard Thy mer-cies as well as Thy severe judgments, and yet have not been effectually moved. Give unto us hearts mollified by Thy Spirit. Look, O Lord, unto Thy children labouring under the imperfections of the flesh, and grant us the victory promised by Jesus Christ Thy Son, our only Saviour, Mediator, and Lawgiver: to Whom, with Thee and the Holy Ghost, be all honour and praise, now and ever. Amen.   KNOX.

Benediction.

The grace of the Lord Jesus Christ, and the love of God, and the communion of the Holy Ghost, be with you all. Amen.

THE FORM

FOR

Ordaining Elders and Deacons.

If ordained separately, this form may be used as occasion shall require.

" *When any person shall have been elected to either of these offices, and shall have declared his willingness to accept thereof, he shall be set apart in the following manner.*

" *After sermon, the Minister shall state, in a concise manner, the warrant and nature of the office of ruling Elder or Deacon, together with the character proper to be sustained and the duties to be fulfilled by the officer elect.*"   DIR. OF WORSHIP.

[The following is a suitable form.]

Beloved Christians, you know that we have several times published unto you the names of our brethren here present who are chosen to the office of Elders and Deacons in this Church, that we might know whether any person had aught to allege why they should not be set apart to their respective offices. And whereas no lawful objection hath been alleged against them, we shall in the Name of the Lord proceed to induct them into the same.

But first we invite your attention to a short declaration from the Word of God, concerning the office and duties of Elders and Deacons. The word ELDER, which is derived from the Old Testament, and signifies a person who is placed in an honourable office of government over others, is applied to two sorts of persons who minister in the Church of Jesus Christ; for the Apostle saith: "The elders that rule well shall be counted worthy of double honour, especially they who labour in the word and doctrine." Hence it is evident that there were two sorts of Elders in the Apostolic Church : the former whereof did labour in the Word and doctrine, and the latter did not. The first were the Ministers of the Word, and Pastors who preached the Word and administered the Sacraments ; but the others, though they did not labour in the Word, yet served the Church by taking the oversight thereof, and ruling the same with the Ministers of the Word. For St. Paul, having spoken of the Ministry of the Word of reconciliation, and also of the office of distribution or Deaconship, speaketh afterwards particularly of this office, saying : "He that ruleth, let him do it with diligence." In another place, he counts "governments" among the gifts and offices which God hath instituted in His Church. In like manner we find the Apostle exhorting the Elders of the Church of Ephesus, to "take heed to themselves and to the flock over which the Holy Ghost had made them overseers."

It is moreover proper that such officers should be joined to the Ministers of the Word in the government of the Church, that there may be no lording over God's heritage ; which can sooner creep in when the government is in the hands of one, or a very few. And thus the Ministers of the Word, together with the Elders, form an Assembly or Council of the Church, representing the whole Body, to which Christ alludes when He saith, "Tell the Church ;" which can in no wise be understood of all and every member of the Church in particular, but very properly of those who govern the Church out of which they are chosen.

Therefore, in the first place, the office of the Elders is, together with the Ministers of the Word, to take the episcopacy or oversight of the Church which is committed to them. In the discharge of their duties, they are to admit to its communion such as profess faith in Christ and repentance for their sins ; diligently to look whether every one properly deports himself in his doctrine and life ; to admonish those who behave disorderly ; to prevent as much as possible the Sacrament from being profaned ; to exercise the discipline of the Church against such as offend ; and to receive them again when penitent to the household of faith.

Secondly, Since the Apostle enjoineth that all things shall be done decently and in order, therefore it is also the duty of the Elders to pay regard to all Christian ordinances ; and in all things which relate to the welfare of the Church, to assist the Ministers of the Word with good counsel, to visit the sick, comfort the afflicted, and to be faithful advisers of all the flock committed to their care.

Thirdly, It is their duty particularly to have regard unto the doctrine and life of the Ministers of the Word, that all things may be directed to the edification of the Church; and that no strange doctrine be taught, according to that which we read where the Apostle exhorteth the Elders to watch diligently against the wolves who might come into the sheepfold of Christ: for the performance of which the Elders are in duty bound diligently to search the Word of God, and continually to be meditating on the mysteries of faith.

Concerning the DEACONS: Of the origin and institution of their office we may read in the sixth chapter of the Acts: where we find that the Apostles themselves did in the beginning serve the poor; At whose feet was brought the price of the things that were sold, and distribution was made unto every man according as he had need. But afterwards, when a murmuring arose, because the widows of the Grecians were neglected in the daily ministration, men were chosen by the advice of the Apostles, who should make the service of the poor their peculiar business: to the end that the Apostles might continually give themselves to prayer, and to the Ministry of the Word. And this has been continued from that time forward in the Church; as appears from Romans xii. where the Apostle speaking of this office saith: "He that giveth, let him do it with simplicity." And speaking of helps, he means those who are appointed in the Church to help and assist the poor and indigent in time of need.

From these passages we may easily gather what the Deacons' office is. In the first place, it is their duty to collect and preserve with the greatest fidelity and diligence the alms which are given to the poor, and that they endeavour that sufficient means be provided for the same. The second part of their office consists in distribution: wherein not only is godly discretion required, to bestow the alms only on the proper objects of charity, but also cheerfulness and simplicity, to assist the poor with becoming sympathy, hearty affection, and also with comfortable words from Scripture—all which the Apostle requires when speaking of the duties of this office.

To the end, therefore, beloved brethren ——, ——, that every one may hear that you are willing to take your respective offices upon you, ye shall answer to the following questions:

"1. Do you believe the Scriptures of the Old and New Testaments to be the Word of God, the only infallible rule of faith and practice?

"2. Do you sincerely receive and adopt the Confession of

Faith of this Church, as containing the system of doctrine taught in the Holy Scriptures?

"3. Do you approve of the government and discipline of the Presbyterian Church in these United States?

"4. Do you accept the office of ruling elder [or deacon, *as the case may be*,] in this congregation, and promise faithfully to perform all the duties thereof?

"5. Do you promise to study the peace, unity, and purity of the Church?

"*The elder or deacon elect having answered these questions in the affirmative, the Minister shall address to the members of the Church the following question:*

"Do you, the members of this Church, acknowledge and receive this brother as a ruling elder, [or deacon,] and do you promise to yield him all that honour, encouragement, and obedience, in the Lord, to which his office, according to the Word of God, and the constitution of this Church, entitles him?

"*The members of the Church having answered this question in the affirmative, by holding up their right hands, the Minister shall proceed to set apart the candidate, by prayer, to the office of ruling elder, or deacon as the case may be.*"

DIR. OF WORSHIP.

[*The following is a suitable form.*]

Prayer.

O Lord God, our Heavenly Father! we thank Thee that it hath pleased Thee, for the better edification of Thy Church, to ordain in it, besides the Ministers of the Word, rulers and assistants, by whom Thy Church may be preserved in peace and prosperity, and the indigent assisted; and that Thou hast at present granted us in this place, men who are of good testimony, and we hope endowed with Thy Spirit. We beseech Thee, replenish them more and more with such gifts as are necessary for them in their ministration; with the gifts of wisdom, courage, discretion, and benevolence; to the end that every one may, in his respective office, acquit himself as is becoming: The Elders, in taking diligent heed unto the doctrine and conversation, in keeping out the wolves from the sheepfold of Thy beloved Son, and in admonishing and reproving disorderly persons. In like manner the deacons, in carefully receiving, and liberally and prudently distributing of the alms to the poor, and in comforting them with Thy holy Word. Give grace both to the elders and deacons, that they may persevere in their faithful labour, and never become weary by reason of any trouble, pain, or persecution of the world. Grant also Thy divine grace to this people over whom they

7

are placed, that they may willingly submit themselves to the good exhortations of the elders, counting them worthy of honour for their work's sake. Give also unto them liberal hearts towards the poor, and to the poor grateful hearts towards those who help and serve them: to the end that every one acquitting himself of his duty, Thy holy Name may thereby be magnified, and the kingdom of Thy Son Jesus Christ enlarged, in whose Name we conclude our prayer.

Our Father which art in heaven, Hallowed be Thy Name. Thy kingdom come. Thy will be done in earth, as it is in heaven. Give us this day our daily bread. And forgive us our debts, as we forgive our debtors. And lead us not into temptation, but deliver us from evil: For Thine is the kingdom, and the power, and the glory, for ever. Amen.

" *The Minister, having set apart the candidate by prayer, shall give to him and to the congregation an exhortation suited to the occasion*

" *Where there is an existing Session, it is proper that the members of that body, at the close of the service, and in the face of the congregation, take the newly-ordained elder by the hand, saying in words to this purpose:*

" We give you the right hand of fellowship, to take part of this office with us."

REFORMED DUTCH LITURGY, *with the exception of the passages marked from the* DIRECTORY OF WORSHIP.

THE FORM

FOR

Ordaining Ministers of the Word of God.

"The day appointed for Ordination being come, and the Presbytery convened, a member of the Presbytery previously appointed to that duty shall preach a sermon adapted to the occasion. The same or another member appointed to preside, shall afterwards briefly recite from the pulpit, in the audience of the people, the proceedings of the Presbytery preparatory to this transaction: he shall point out the nature and importance of the ordinance; and endeavour to impress the audience with a proper sense of the solemnity of the transaction." DIR. OF WORSHIP.

[The following is an appropriate form.]

Beloved brethren, attend to a short declaration taken from the holy Scriptures touching the Ministry of reconciliation and the Pastoral office.

We are not to look for the origin of this office in human appointment, but in God, our Heavenly Father, who, being willing to call and gather a Church from among the corrupt race of men into life eternal, doth by a particular mark of His favour, use the ministry of men therein. Accordingly, our Lord Jesus Christ, shortly before His ascension to heaven, gave to His Apostles the commission, "Go ye therefore and teach all nations, baptizing them in the Name of the Father, and of the Son, and of the Holy Ghost: and lo! I am with you alway even unto the end of the world." Therefore St. Paul saith that the "Lord Jesus Christ hath given some Apostles and some Prophets and some Evangelists and some Pastors and Teachers: for the perfecting of the saints, for the work of the Ministry, for the edifying of the Body of Christ." Thus we see that the Pastoral office is an institution of Christ.

In the Ministry, thus divinely appointed, there is no superi-

oi ity of rank or diversity of order; but all are possessed of the
same authority, dignity, and power: being equally clothed
with the right of preaching the Gospel, of administering the
Sacraments and discipline of Christ's house, and of ordaining
others to the same office.

What this holy office of Pastor enjoins, may easily be
gathered from the very name itself: for, as it is the duty of the
shepherd to feed, guide, protect, and rule the flock committed
to his charge, so it is with regard to these spiritual shepherds
who are set over the Church which God calleth unto salvation,
and accounts as sheep of His pasture. .

The pasture with which these sheep are fed is the Preaching
of the Gospel, accompanied with prayer and the administration
of the holy Sacraments. The same Word of God is likewise
the staff with which the flock is guided and ruled. Therefore
the office of Pastors and Ministers of God's Word is—

First. That they shall faithfully explain to their flocks the
Word of the Lord, revealed by the writings of the Prophets
and Apostles, and apply the same to the edification of the hear-
ers; instructing, admonishing, comforting, and reproving according to every one's need, preaching repentance towards God
and reconciliation to Him through faith in Christ; and refuting
from the holy Scriptures all schisms and heresies which are
repugnant to the pure doctrine. All this is clearly signified to
us in holy writ, for the Apostle Paul saith that these "labour in
the Word," and elsewhere he teacheth that this must be done
"according to the measure or rule of faith." He writes also
that a Pastor "must rightly divide the Word of Truth." In
another place he proposes himself as a pattern to Pastors, declaring that he hath "publicly from house to house taught and
testified repentance towards God and faith towards our Lord
Jesus Christ." But particularly we have a clear description of
their office, where the Apostle thus speaketh : "And all things
are of God, who hath reconciled us to Himself, by Jesus Christ,
and hath given to us the Ministry of reconciliation: to wit,
that God was in Christ, reconciling the world unto Himself, not
imputing their trespasses unto them, and hath committed unto
us the Word of reconciliation. Now then we are embassadors
for Christ, as though God did beseech you by us ; we pray you
in Christ's stead, be ye reconciled to God."

So also concerning the refutation of false doctrine, the same
Apostle saith, that a Minister must "hold fast the faithful
Word of God as he hath been taught, that he may be able by
sound doctrine both to exhort and to convince the gainsayers."

Secondly. It is the office of the Ministers publicly to call upon
the Name of the Lord in behalf of the whole Congregation.
For that which the Apostles say, "We will give ourselves con-

tinually to prayer and to the Ministry of the Word," is common to these Pastors with the Apostles: to which St. Paul alluding speaketh thus to Timothy: "I exhort, therefore, that first of all, supplications, prayers, intercessions, and giving of thanks be made for all men; for kings and for all who are in authority, that we may lead a quiet and peaceable life in all godliness and honesty; for this is good and acceptable in the sight of God our Saviour."

Thirdly. Their office is to administer the Sacraments which the Lord hath instituted as seals of His grace. As is evident from the command given by Christ to the Apostles, and in them to all Pastors: " Baptize them in the Name of the Father and of the Son and of the Holy Ghost." Likewise the Apostle speaking of the institution of the Lord's Supper saith, "For I have received of the Lord that which also I delivered unto you."

Finally. It is the duty of the Ministers of the Word, together with the other Elders, to maintain the discipline of the Church; and to govern it in such manner as the Lord hath ordained. For Christ having spoken of the Christian discipline, says to His Apostles: "Whatsoever ye shall bind on earth shall be bound in heaven." This is the reason why the Pastors are in Scripture called " Stewards of God," and " Bishops," for they have the oversight of the house of God, to the end that every thing may be done decently and in order; and also have authority to open and shut with the keys committed to them the Kingdom of Heaven, according to the charge given them by God.

From these things may be learned what a glorious work the ministerial office is; yea, how highly necessary it is for man's salvation: which is also the reason why the Lord wills that such an office should always remain. For Christ said when He sent forth His Apostles to officiate in this holy function, " Lo! I am with you always, even unto the end of the world;" where we see His pleasure is, that this holy office should always be maintained on earth. And therefore St. Paul exhorteth Timothy, to " commit that which he had heard of him to faithful men who are able to teach others:" as he also, having ordained Titus a minister, further commanded him " to ordain elders in every city." (Tit. 1 : 5.)

Forasmuch therefore as we, for the maintaining of this office in the Church of God, are now to ordain a new Minister of the Word, and have sufficiently spoken of the office of such persons, therefore you, beloved brother N., shall answer to the following questions which shall be proposed to you, to the end that it may appear to all here present that you are inclined to accept this office as it has been described.

" 1. Do you believe the Scriptures of the Old and New Testaments to be the Word of God, the only infallible rule of faith
and practice ?

" 2. Do you sincerely receive and adopt the Confession of
Faith of this Church as containing the system of doctrine taught
in the Holy Scriptures ?

" 3. Do you approve of the government and discipline of
the Presbyterian Church in these United States ?

" 4. Do you promise subjection to your brethren in the
Lord ?

" 5. Have you been induced, as far as you know your own
heart, to seek the office of the holy Ministry from love to
God, and a sincere desire to promote His glory in the Gospel
of His Son ?

" 6. Do you promise to be zealous and faithful in maintaining
the truths of the Gospel, and the purity and peace of the Church:
whatever persecution or opposition may arise unto you on that
account?

" " 7. Do you engage to be faithful and diligent in the exercise of all private and personal duties, which become you as a
Christian and a Minister of the Gospel ; as well as in all rela-
tive duties, and the public duties of your office : endeavouring
to adorn the profession of the Gospel by your conversation ;
and walking with exemplary piety before the flock over which
God shall make you overseer ?

" [8. Are you now willing to take the charge of this congregation, agreeably to your declaration at accepting their call ?
And do you promise to discharge the duties of a Pastor to them,
as God shall give you strength?]

" *The Candidate having answered these [questions in the affirmative, [the Presiding
Minister shall propose to the people the following questions :*

" 1. Do you, the people of this congregation, continue to
profess your readiness to receive —— ——, whom you have
called to be your Minister ?

" 2. Do you promise to receive the Word of truth from his
mouth, with meekness and love ; and to submit to him in the
due exercise of discipline?

" 3. Do you promise to encourage him in his arduous labour,
and to assist his endeavours for your instruction and spiritual
edification ?

" 4. And do you engage to continue to him, while he is your
Pastor, that competent worldly maintenance which you have
promised ; and whatever else you may see needful for the honour of religion, and his comfort among you ?]

" The people having answered these questions in the affirmative, by holding up their right hands,] the Candidate shall kneel down in the most convenient part of the church. Then the Presiding Minister shall, by prayer, and with the laying on of the hands of the Presbytery, according to the Apostolic example, solemnly ordain him to the holy office of the Gospel Ministry."

" As it is sometimes desirable and important that a candidate who has not received a call to be the pastor of a particular congregation, should nevertheless be ordained to the work of the Gospel ministry, as an Evangelist to preach the Gospel, administer Sealing Ordinances, and organize churches, in frontier or destitute settlements; in this case, the last of the preceding questions [and the questions to the people] shall be omitted, and the following used as a substitute : viz.

" Are you now willing to undertake the work of an Evangelist; and do you promise to discharge the duties which may be incumbent on you in this character, as God shall give you strength ?"
Dir. of Worship.

The following is a suitable form for

The Ordaining Prayer.

O Lord, to whom all power is given in heaven and in earth ! Thou art the Eternal Son of the Father; who hast so loved Thy Church, that to redeem and purify it Thou didst humble Thyself to the death of the Cross, and there shed Thy most innocent blood. And to retain this Thy most excellent benefit in memory, Thou hast appointed in Thy Church pastors and teachers, to instruct, admonish, and comfort Thy people. Look upon us mercifully, O Lord, Thou only King, Teacher, and High Priest to Thine own flock ; and send unto this Thy servant our brother, whom in Thy name we set apart and ordain, such a portion of Thy Holy Spirit, that he may rightly divide Thy Word, to the instruction of Thy flock, and the overthrow of error and vice. Give unto him, good Lord, Thy grace and wisdom, whereby the enemies of Thy truth may be confounded, the blind and ignorant edified, and Thy sheep fed in the wholesome pastures of Thy most holy Word. Multiply Thy graces upon him. Illuminate him with Thine Holy Spirit. Comfort and strengthen him in all virtue. Govern and guide his ministry, to the praise of Thy holy Name, the promotion of Thy kingdom, the comfort of Thy Church, and to the plain discharge of his own conscience in the day of the Lord Jesus : To Whom, with the Father and with the Holy Ghost, be all honour, praise, and glory, now and ever. Amen.
Knox.

" Prayer being ended, he shall rise from his knees; and the Minister who presides shall first, and afterward all the members of the Presbytery in their order, take him by the right hand, saying, in words to this purpose,

" We give you the right hand of fellowship, to take part of this ministry with us.

" After which the Minister presiding, or some other appointed for the purpose, shall give a solemn charge in the Name of God to the newly-ordained Bishop, and to the people, to persevere in the discharge of their mutual duties."

Charge to the Newly-Ordained Minister, and the Congregation.

Take heed, therefore, beloved brother, and fellow-servant in Christ, unto yourself and to all the flock, over which the Holy Ghost hath made you overseer, to feed the Church of God which He hath purchased with His own blood. Love Christ, and feed His sheep, taking the oversight of them not by constraint, but willingly; not for filthy lucre, but of a ready mind, neither as being lord over God's heritage, but as an example to the flock. Be an example of believers, in word, in conversation, in charity, in spirit, in faith, in purity. Give attendance to reading, to exhortation, to doctrine. Neglect not the gift that is in thee, meditate upon those things, give thyself wholly to them, that thy profiting may appear to all: take heed to thy doctrine, and continue stedfast therein. Bear patiently all sufferings and oppressions, as a good soldier of Jesus Christ, for in doing this thou shalt both save thyself and them that hear thee. And when the chief Shepherd shall appear, thou shalt receive a crown of glory that fadeth not away.

And you likewise, beloved Christians, receive this your Minister in the Lord with all gladness, "and hold such in reputation." Remember that God Himself through him speaketh unto you and beseecheth you. Receive the Word, which he, according to the Scripture, shall preach unto you, "not as the word of man, but (as it is in truth) the Word of God." Let the feet of those that preach the Gospel of peace, and bring glad tidings of good things, be beautiful and pleasant unto you. Obey them that have the rule over you, and submit yourselves; for they watch for your souls, as they that must give account, that they may do it with joy and not with grief; for that is unprofitable for you. If you do these things, it shall come to pass, that the peace of God shall enter into your houses, and that you who receive this man in the name of a prophet, shall receive a prophet's reward, and through his preaching, believing in Christ, shall through Christ inherit life eternal.

" Then the Presiding Minister shall, by prayer, recommend both the newly-ordained Minister and the congregation, to the grace of God, and His holy keeping."

Prayer.

Merciful Father, we thank Thee that it pleaseth Thee, by the ministry of men, to gather a Church to Thyself unto life eternal, from amongst the lost children of men. We bless Thee for so graciously providing the Church in this place with a faithful Minister. We beseech Thee to qualify him daily more and more by the Holy Spirit, for the ministry to which Thou hast ordained and called him: enlighten his understanding to comprehend Thy holy Word, and give him utterance, that he may boldly open his mouth, to make known and dispense the mysteries of the Gospel. Endue him with wisdom and valour, to rule the people aright over which he is set, and to preserve them in Christian peace, to the end that Thy Church under his administration and by his good example, may increase in number and in virtue. Grant him courage to bear the difficulties and troubles which he may meet with in his ministry, that being strengthened by the comfort of Thy Spirit, he may remain stedfast to the end, and be received with all faithful servants into the joy of his Master. Give Thy grace also to this people and Church, that they may becomingly deport themselves towards this their Minister; that they may acknowledge him to be sent of Thee; that they may receive his doctrine with all reverence, and submit themselves to his exhortations: To the end that they may, by his Word, believing in Christ, be made partakers of eternal life. Hear us, O Father, through Thy beloved Son, who hath thus taught us to pray—OUR FATHER, etc.

" Finally, after singing a Psalm, he shall dismiss the congregation with the usual "

Blessing.

The grace of the Lord Jesus Christ, and the love of God, and the Communion of the Holy Ghost, be with you all. Amen.   REFORMED DUTCH LITURGY *and* DIRECTORY OF WORSHIP.

PRAYERS OF THE APOSTLES.

A Thanksgiving.

Blessed be Thou, O God and Father of our Lord Jesus Christ, Who hast blessed us with all spiritual blessings in heavenly places in Christ: according as Thou hast chosen us in Him before the foundation of the world, that we should be holy and without blame before Thee in love: and hast predestinated us unto the adoption of children by Jesus Christ to Thyself, according to the good pleasure of Thy will. We praise the glory of Thy grace, wherein Thou hast made us accepted in the Beloved. We bless Thee that in Him we have redemption through His blood, the forgiveness of sins, according to the riches of Thy grace. We bless Thee for making known to us the mystery of Thy will: that in the dispensation of the fulness of times Thou mightest gather together all things in Christ, both which are in heaven and which are on earth, even in Him. And we give thanks unto Thee, O Lord! for the faith and love of all Thy saints: beseeching Thee that they, having heard the Gospel of their salvation, and trusted in Christ, may be sealed with that Holy Spirit of Promise, which is the earnest of their inheritance, until the redemption of the purchased possession, to the praise of Thy glory. Amen.

EPH. I. 3–16.

A Prayer for Wisdom.

O God of our Lord Jesus Christ, the Father of Glory! Give unto us the Spirit of wisdom and revelation in the knowledge of Him: that the eyes of our understanding may be enlightened: that we may know what is the hope of His calling, and what the riches of the glory of His inheritance in the saints. Manifest, O Lord! the exceeding greatness of Thy power to us-ward who believe, according to its mighty working in Christ, when Thou didst raise Him from the dead, and settest Him at Thine own right hand in the heavenly places, far above all principality, and power, and might, and dominion, and every name that is named, not only in this world, but also in that which is to come. EPH. I. 17–21.

For Spiritual Strength.

O Father of our Lord Jesus Christ, of Whom the whole Family in heaven and earth is named: We bow our knees unto Thee, beseeching that Thou wilt grant us, according to the riches of Thy glory, to be strengthened with might by Thy Spirit in the inner man: That Christ may dwell in our hearts by faith: That we, being rooted and grounded in love, may be able to comprehend with all saints, what is the breadth and length and depth and height, and to know the love of Christ, that passeth knowledge; that we may be filled with all the fulness of God. Now unto Him that is able to do exceeding abundantly above all that we ask or think, according to the power that worketh in us, unto Him be glory in the Church by Christ Jesus throughout all ages, world without end. Amen. EPH. III. 14–21.

For a Good Judgment.

Almighty God, we pray Thee, that the love of all Thy People may abound yet more and more, in knowledge and in all judgment: that they may approve those things which are excellent: that they may be sincere and without offence till the day of Christ; being filled with the fruits of righteousness which are by Jesus Christ, unto the glory and praise of God. PHILIP. I. 9–11.

For the Prosperity of the Church.

O God and Father of our Lord Jesus Christ, we give Thee thanks for all Thy saints our faithful brethren in Christ throughout the earth: desiring that they might all be filled with the knowledge of Thy will, in all wisdom and spiritual understanding; that they might walk worthy of the Lord unto all pleasing, being fruitful in every good work, and increasing in the knowledge of God. Strengthen them with all might, according to Thy glorious power, unto all patience and long-suffering with joyfulness. May they ever give thanks unto Thee, O Father: who hast made us meet to be partakers of the inheritance of the saints in light; who hast delivered us from the power of darkness, and hast translated us into the kingdom of Thy dear Son, in Whom we have redemption through His blood, even the forgiveness of sins. COL. I. 1–13.

For Faith and Charity.

O God, we render thanks unto Thee for the faith and charity of Thy People, and the joy wherewith we joy for their sakes before Thee. And we beseech Thee to perfect that which is yet lacking in their faith. Make them to increase and abound in love toward one another, and toward all men: to the end that their hearts may be established unblameable in holiness before God even our Father, at the coming of our Lord Jesus Christ with all His saints. O Thou very God of peace, sanctify them wholly; and may their whole spirit, and soul, and body, be preserved blameless unto the coming of our Lord Jesus Christ. Amen.   1 THESS. III. 6-13; v. 23.

A Prayer for Rulers and Ministers.

O God, who hast exhorted us by Thine Apostle to make supplications, prayers, intercessions, and giving of thanks, for all men: We pray for kings, and all that are in authority; that we may lead a quiet and peaceable life in all godliness and holiness. We also pray for all Thy servants, who in every place make manifest the savour of Thy knowledge, preaching among the nations the unsearchable riches of Christ. Supply them with Thy Spirit; give utterance unto them to make known the mystery of the Gospel; open unto them doors of utterance; deliver them from unreasonable and wicked men: and may the Word of the Lord have free course and be glorified, even as it is with us.

1 Ti. ii. 1-2; 1 Thess. v. 25; 2 Cor. ii. 14; Eph. iii. 8; Phil. i. 19; Eph. vi. 19; Col. iv. 3; 2 Thess. iii. 2; id. 1.

For Sanctification.

Vouchsafe, O our God! we pray Thee, to count us worthy of Thy calling, and to fulfil all the good pleasure of Thy goodness, and the work of faith with power: That the Name of our Lord Jesus Christ may be glorified in us, and we in Him, according to the grace of our God and the Lord Jesus Christ. Amen.   2 THESS. I. 11, 12.

For Stedfastness.

O God! Who from the beginning hast chosen us to salvation through sanctification of the Spirit, and belief of the Truth: Grant us grace to stand fast, and hold the traditions which we have been taught, to the obtaining of the glory of our Lord Jesus Christ. O Lord Jesus Christ! who Thyself hast loved us, and hast given us everlasting consolation, and good hope through grace: Comfort our hearts, and establish us in every good word and work.   2 THESS. II. 13-17.

For Grace to do Good Works.

O God of Peace! who broughtest again from the dead our Lord Jesus, that great Shepherd of the sheep, through the blood of the everlasting Covenant: Make us perfect in every good work to do Thy will, working in us that which is well-pleasing in Thy sight: Through Jesus Christ, to Whom be glory for ever and ever. Amen. HEB. XIII. 20, 21.

For Perseverance.

God of all Grace! Who hast called us unto Thine eternal glory by Christ Jesus: Make us perfect, stablish, strengthen, settle us; that God in all things may be glorified, through Jesus Christ, to Whom be praise and dominion for ever and ever. Amen. 1 PETER V. 10; IV. 11.

For Unity.

O God of Patience and Consolation, grant us to be like-minded one toward another according to Christ Jesus: that we may with one mind and one mouth glorify Thee, the Father of our Lord Jesus Christ. ROM. XV. 5, 6.

For Hope.

O God of Hope, fill us with all joy and peace in believing, that we may abound in hope, through the power of the Holy Ghost. ROM. XV. 13.

Ascriptions of Praise.

Now to God only Wise be glory through Jesus Christ for ever. Amen. ROM. XVI. 27.

Now unto the King Eternal, Immortal, Invisible, the only Wise God, be honour and glory for ever and ever. Amen. 1 TI. I. 17.

Now to the Blessed and Only Potentate, the King of kings, and Lord of lords; Who only hath immortality, dwelling in the light which no man can approach unto, Whom no man hath seen nor can see: To Him be honour and power everlasting. Amen. 1 TI. IV. 15, 16.

Now unto Him that is able to keep us from falling, and to present us faultless before the presence of His glory with exceeding joy: To the only Wise God our Saviour, be glory and majesty, dominion and power, both now and ever. Amen. JUDE 24, 25.

AN ORDER

FOR THE

Reading of Scripture in Public Worship.

READING OF THE WORD IN THE CONGREGATION, BEING PART OF THE PUBLIC WOR-
SHIP OF GOD, WHEREIN WE ACKNOWLEDGE OUR DEPENDENCE UPON HIM AND SUB-
JECTION TO HIM, AND ONE MEANS SANCTIFIED BY HIM FOR THE EDIFYING OF HIS
PEOPLE, IS TO BE PERFORMED BY THE PASTOR AND TEACHER.

HOW LARGE A PORTION SHALL BE READ AT ONCE, IS LEFT TO THE WISDOM OF THE
MINISTER: BUT IT IS CONVENIENT THAT ORDINARILY ONE CHAPTER OF EACH TESTA-
MENT BE READ AT EVERY MEETING; AND SOMETIMES MORE, WHERE THE CHAPTERS
BE SHORT, OR THE COHERENCE OF MATTER REQUIRETH IT.

IT IS REQUISITE THAT ALL THE CANONICAL BOOKS BE READ OVER IN ORDER, THAT
THE PEOPLE MAY BE BETTER ACQUAINTED WITH THE WHOLE BODY OF THE SCRIPTURES:
AND ORDINARILY, WHERE THE READING IN EITHER TESTAMENT ENDETH ON ONE
LORD'S DAY, IT IS TO BEGIN THE NEXT

Directory for Worship, by the Westminster Divines: § 2.

The following Order has been prepared to facilitate selection.

Sun-days.	MORNING SERVICE.		EVENING SERVICE	
	First Portion.	Second.	First Portion.	Second
1	Gen i.	John i 1–18	Isa. i. 1–20.	Acts ii. 1–21.
2	ii.	Luke i 26–56.	ii.	ii. 22–47.
3	iii	Matt. i.	v. 1–17.	vi.
4	vi.	Luke ii. 1–20.	vi.	ix. 1–22.
5	vii.	Matt. ii.	vii. 10–25.	xi. 1–18.
6	viii.	John i 19–51	ix	xvi. 14–40.
7	ix 1–19.	Matt. iv.	xi.	xxvi.
8	xii.	John iii. 1–21.	xxv.	Rom i. 1–25.
9	xxii.	John iv. 1–26.	xxvi.	iv.
10	xxviii.	Luke iv. 16–37.	xxxv.	v.
11	xxxvii. 1–28.	Luke v. 1–26.	xxxviii.	vi.
12	xlii 1–28.	John v. 19–47.	xl.	vii.
13	xliii.	Matt. xii. 1–21.	xli.	viii.
14	xlv.	Matt. v 1–20.	xlii.	xii.
15	xlvi. 1–7; 28–34; and xlvii. 1–12.	Matt vi 1–18.	xliii.	xv. 1–13.
16	xlviii.	Matt. vi. 19–34.	xliv.	1 Cor. i 1–25.

	MORNING SERVICE.		EVENING SERVICE.	
Sun-days	First Portion.	Second	First Portion.	Second
17	Gen. xlix.	Matt vii.	Isa. xlv.	1 Cor. ii.
18	Ex. ii.	Matt xi.	xlviii	iii.
19	iii.	Matt xii. 1–21.	xlix.	xii.
20	v.	Matt. xiii. 1–30.	li.	xiii.
21	xii. 1–36.	Matt. xiii. 33–58.	lii	xiv. 1–20.
22	xiv.	Matt. ix. 18–38.	liii.	xv. 1–20.
23	xv.	Matt. x. 1–20.	liv.	xv. 21–58.
24	xvi. 1–19.	Matt. xiv. 14–36.	lv.	2 Cor. iv.
25	xl 17–38.	John vi. 35–59.	lviii.	v.
26	Deut.i. 19–46.	Matt xvi.	lix.	vi
27	iv. 23–40.	Matt. xvii 1–21.	lx.	Gal iii.
28	ix.	Matt. xviii. 1–20.	lxi.	Eph i.
29	xviii.	Luke x. 1–24.	lxii.	ii.
30	xxxiii.	John vii 14–31.	lxiii.	iii
31	Josh. iii.	John vii. 32–52.	lxiv.	iv.
32	vii.	Luke x. 25–42.	lxv.	v.
33	xxiv 1–25.	Luke xi. 1–13.	lxvi.	Philip. ii. 1–18.
34	Judg. ii.	Luke xii 1–21.	Jer. xiv. 7–22.	Col. iii.
35	Ruth i.	Luke xii. 22–48.	xvii. 5–27.	1 Thes v.
36	1Sam.iii.	John ix. 1–25.	xxxi. 1–20.	2 Thes.ii.
37	xii.	John x. 1–18.	xxxiii 1–16.	Heb. i.
38	xv. 1–23.	John xi. 19–46.	Lam. iii. 22–59.	ii.
39	xvi 1–13.	John xii. 12–36.	Ezek. i.	iii.
40	2Sam.vii.	John xiii.	x.	iv.
41	xii. 1–23.	John xiv.	xxxiii 1–20.	x
42	1 Ki. iii. 1–15.	John xv.	xxxiv. 11–31.	xi.
43	vi 11–38.	John xvi	xxxvii 1–14.	xii.
44	ix. 1–14.	John xvii.	xliii. 1–12.	James ii.
45	xvii.	John xviii. 1–27.	xlvii. 1–12.	1 Pet ii.
46	xviii. 17–46.	Luke xxiii. 1–25.	Dan. iii.	1 John v.
47	xix.	Luke xxii 26–49.	vi.	Revel. i
48	2 Ki. ii.	John xix. 25–42.	ix.	iii.
49	v. 1–19.	John xx. 1–18.	Amos v. 1–15.	v.
50	2 Ch. xxxvi. 1–21.	Luke xxiv. 13–35.	Mic. iv.	xix.
51	Neh. viii.	John xx. 19–31.	Hab. iii.	xx.
52	Job i.	John xx. xxi.	Zech. xii.	xxi.
53	xlii.	Acts i. 1–14.	Mal. iii.	xxii.

NOTES.

THE OPENING SENTENCES: Pp. 3, 22 —Calvin's Liturgy introduces the ordinary Service for the Lord's Day, with a sentence of Scripture. Hence a similar feature in the Book of Common Prayer Instead of the single passage (Psalm cxxiv. 8) with which Calvin begins, we have preferred to give several passages for selection: being such as contain appropriate promises of Divine presence to worshipping assemblies. Isaiah lxvi 1, 2; Isaiah lvii. 15; Isaiah lvi. 6, 7; Exodus xx. 24; St Matt. xviii. 20; St John xiv. 13; Hebrews ix. 24.

INVITATION: Page 4 —The invitation in the French Liturgy reads thus: "*My brethren, let each of you present himself before the Lord, in order to make an humble confession of his sins unto Him: following in heart these words*" The Middleburgh Prayer-book has it thus "*Let us fall down before the majesty of Almighty God, humbly confessing our sins; and follow in your hearts the tenour of my words.*" In place of these forms, we have used Scriptural language combining the passages, 2 Cor. vii. 1; Heb. x. 22; Phil iv. 6; and in addition, Heb. iv. 16

BUCER'S LITANY: Page 26.—This beautiful prayer, modelled upon the ancient litanies, yet possessing much originality and peculiar beauty, is due, in all probability, to the Reformer Bucer; from whose "Reformation of Doctrine and Worship," it is literally translated. The Litany of the English Prayer-Book is for the most part borrowed from this form.

THE MARRIAGE SERVICE: Page 76 —Of the two forms given for this ordinance, the one is compiled from the Liturgies of Geneva, Scotland, and Holland The other is extracted from the Proposed Liturgy of the Reformed Dutch Church in America.

THE BURIAL SERVICE: Page 81.—The Liturgies of the Reformed Churches on the Continent supply us with few examples of a service for Burial. The danger of superstitious observances, at the period when those formularies were compiled, deterred Calvin and others from furnishing any prescribed order. It has always been customary to consecrate the last offices at the grave with prayer but for this, even, the French Liturgy gives no form.
Martin Bucer was the author of a service for the Burial of the Dead, which is to be found in Herman's Reformation of Cologne This service the English Reformers partly followed. The selections of Scripture, from St. John xi, Psalm xc, and 1 Cor. xv, are there indicated. But Bucer's form possesses a merit of adaptation which is wanting to that of the Anglican Church; for in addition to the services for adults, there is an "*Alia Concio in Funere Adolescentis, vel Adolescentulæ.*" The words of sepulture are taken from Bucer's "Postquam sic visum est Omnipotenti Deo, ut hunc fratrem nostrum pro sua misericordia ex hoc mundo sublatum ad se reciperet," etc.
The present Form of Burial is borrowed from the revision of the Reformed Dutch Liturgy, prepared by a committee under appointment of the General Synod. The selection of Scripture is the best that we have seen. Three services are provided for · a short one at the house, a principal one at the church, and a form of interment. The prayer concluding the service at the church, is from Jeremy Taylor, it has been introduced into the American edition of the Book of Common Prayer.

Date Due

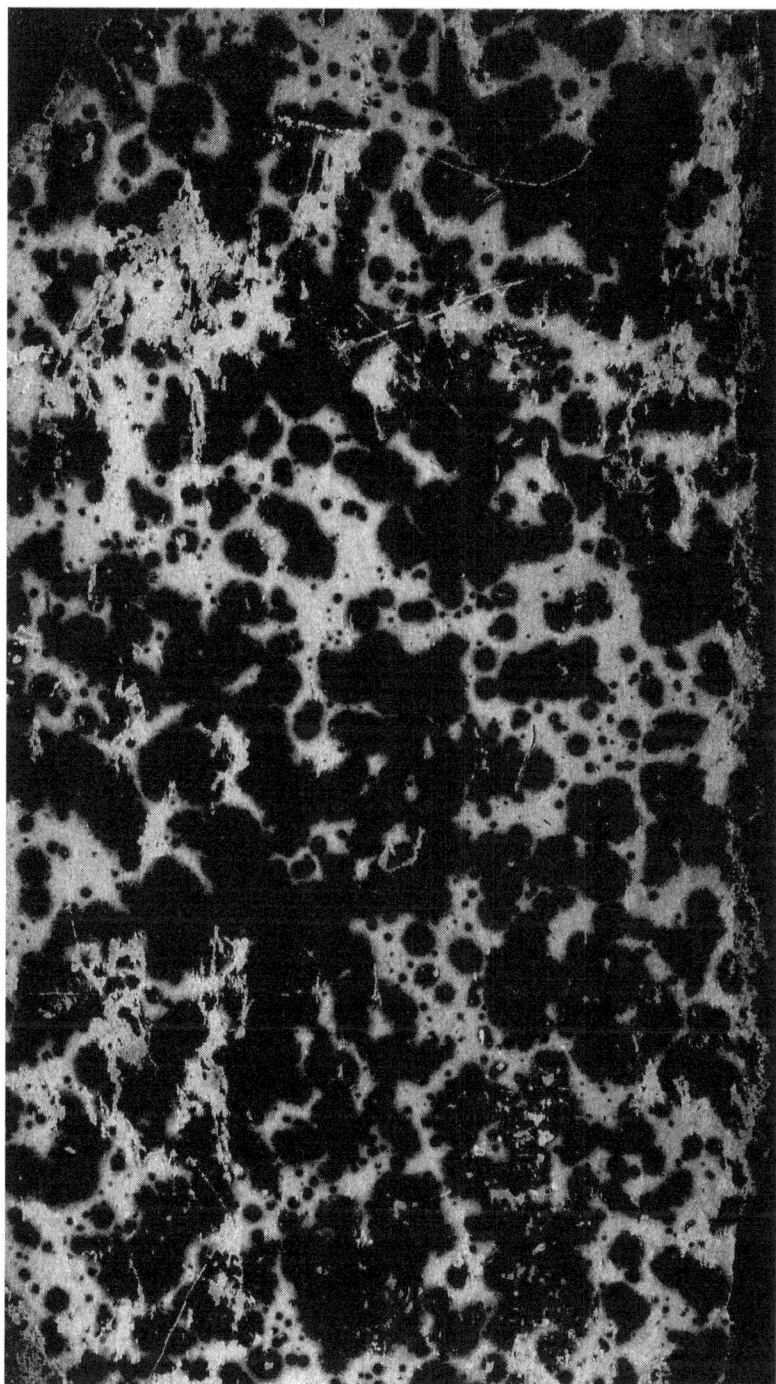

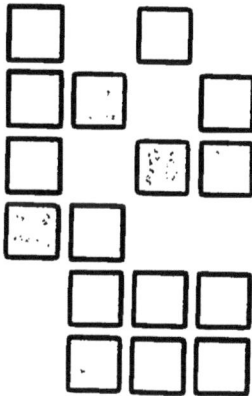

Lightning Source UK Ltd.
Milton Keynes UK
UKHW021952150722
405935UK00003B/50